DATE DUE

THE STRANGERS

The Tragic World of Tristan L'Hermite

by Claude K. Abraham

UNIVERSITY OF FLORIDA PRESS / GAINESVILLE, 1966

AUTHOR'S NOTE

Professor Jerome Schweitzer and I, in preparing a forthcoming edition of the plays of Tristan, compared all the editions of these plays and decided that the following were the most reliable:

La Mariane (Paris: Courbé, 1637), the second (in-4) edition;

Panthée (Paris: Courbé, 1639), the second (in-12) edition;

La folie du sage (Paris: Quinet, 1645), the first edition;

La mort de Sénèque (Paris: Quinet, 1645), the first edition;

La mort de Chrispe (Paris: Besongne, 1645), the first edition;

Amarillis (Paris: de Luine, 1653), the second (in-12) edition;

Le Parasite (Paris: Courbé, 1654), the
   only edition;
Osman (Paris: de Luynes, 1656), the
   only edition.

It is from these editions that the quotations cited by line numbers in this monograph are taken. I have, however, taken the liberty of modernizing the spelling and the punctuation, except in cases where such changes might have endangered the meaning or interfered with the poetry.

I would like to express my gratitude to Professor J. Wayne Conner, for his encouragement in the undertaking of this study; to Mr. Ray Jones, for his help in locating some rare materials; to Professor Jerome Schweitzer and M. Amédée Carriat, whose love of Tristan has been a constant inspiration; and to Marcia, without whose patient ministering to the author and his *brouillons* this study could not have come to fruition.

C. K. A.

July, 1966

CONTENTS

INTRODUCTION

Tristan L'Hermite, in spite of several recent studies, has not yet been accorded the rank he deserves among seventeenth-century dramatists. This is due in large part to the presence of giants such as Corneille and Racine, but much of the blame must be shouldered by the critics who have insisted on denying Tristan an identity of his own and on making of him a follower or a precursor of one school—or individual—or another.

In this study, an attempt has been made, after a few preliminary pages, to approach the work of Tristan not by comparing it to that of others, not by categorizing it, but by means of character analysis. This analysis may be considered by some too heavily based on existential criteria, but the anachronism is only a tool of investigation that may help in our understanding of the author without infringing on his integrity.

Using a formula already set forth by Ernest Serret,[1] N.-M. Bernardin, in his monumental thesis that remains, in spite of the years, the basic *vie et œuvre* of Tristan, suggests that Tristan is a precursor of classical tragedy.[2] Antoine Adam[3] and Jacques Scherer[4] consider him more a successor of Garnier than a precursor of Racine. They suggest that Tristan is not even an innovator in the realm of dramatic structure, since his first play comes after Mairet's *Sophonisbe*, the pio-

---

1. "Un précurseur de Racine," *Le Correspondent* (April 25, 1870), pp. 334-54.
2. *Un précurseur de Racine: Tristan L'Hermite, sieur du Solier (1601-1655), sa famille, sa vie, ses œuvres* (Paris: Picard, 1895).
3. *Histoire de la littérature française au XVIIe siècle* (Paris: Daumat, 1962), I, 544-48.
4. *La dramaturgie classique en France* (Paris: Nizet, 1950), *passim*.

1

neer in that field. According to several critics, Tristan owes a genuine debt to the Elizabethan dramatists. In order to ascertain the value of any or all of these positions, it is necessary to separate problems which, it seems to us, have been treated as one entity.

Let us consider, for instance, the introduction by Georges May to an edition of *Polyeucte* and *Le menteur*, in which he states quite clearly: "It is hardly surprising . . . that a play like *Polyeucte*—labeled in 1660 *tragédie chrétienne*—should appear to us neither tragic nor Christian."[5] A short while later, he adds: "*Polyeucte* cannot be considered a tragedy if we define tragedy in terms of *Œdipus-Rex*, *Othello*, or *Phèdre*. Yet, as a play, *Polyeucte* does fit the less metaphysical concept of tragedy prevalent in mid-seventeenth-century France: a serious five-act play, written in an elevated style and in alexandrines; with protagonists of noble blood engaged in a significant action, at least one of whom loses his life by the time the play ends" (pp. 24-25). These two statements raise several basic points: Is tragedy basically tragic? Is a tragedy, in mid-seventeenth-century France, merely what Mr. May suggests?

In order to answer these two questions, it might be well to recall, however briefly and sketchily, what the words "tragic" and "tragedy" meant to the authors of that time. We do not wish to deny the value of absolute standards, nor do we mean to imply that great profit cannot be derived from applying to a creative author criteria which he ignored, but Corneille called his *Cid* a "tragi-comédie" in the beginning, changing it to "tragédie" in 1648; by the same token, *Polyeucte*, a "tragédie" in 1643, became a "tragédie chrétienne" in 1660; labels do have a meaning and are valuable only insofar as that meaning is specific and helps us in identifying the item labeled. First then, what is a tragedy in mid-seventeenth-

5. (New York: Dell, 1963), p. 24.

century France? May we accept Mr. May's definition? Hardly: *Esther* is in three acts, La Serre writes his tragedies exclusively in prose—and is extremely popular—and in an often pedestrian language, and no one dies in *Bérénice*.

Aristotle admitted a happy ending in tragedy, but Scaliger did not, adding to the original "imitatio per actiones illustris fortunae" his own "exitu infelici."[6] Castelvetro agreed with the latter in his *Poetica d'Aristotele vulgarizzata e sposta*. In 1598, in his *Art poétique français*, Pierre de Laudun d'Aigaliers put these same ideas into French, and Vossius, half a century later, altered little in that definition: "Praecipuum ac essentiale discrimen est quod in tragœdia sit illustris personarum illustrium actio, terrorem continens ac misericordiam."[7] Corneille, at the time of the writing of *Don Sanche*, attacked such separation of genres, and for good cause: the noble characters of his play are involved in a very comic situation; ten years later, he was again in agreement with the aforementioned critics.[8]

Let us now look at the work of the dramatists themselves, to find to what extent they followed the rules set down by the critics in three of the basic areas, i.e., in the treatment of action, of characters, and of passions.[9]

Aristotle had noted that tragedy was usually based on a historical subject. Chapelain asserted that "beaucoup de spéculatifs en cette doctrine ont estimé que la vraisemblance, qui d'ailleurs fait l'essence de la poésie dans le particulier du poème tragique, ne suffirait pas pour lui bailler fondement et qu'une tragédie ne se pouvait dire absolument bonne qui n'eût

---

6. *Poeticae septem libri* (Bib. Commeliano, 1617), p. 25.

7. *De artis poeticae natura* . . . (Amsterdam: Elzévir, 1647), II, 112.

8. René Bray, *La formation de la doctrine classique en France* (Lausanne: Payot, 1931), p. 308.

9. It is important to note here that, while Aristotle merely wished to help the public to understand past and present dramatists by explaining the "why" of their success or of their failure, the European critics of the sixteenth and seventeenth centuries thought of themselves as teachers of present and future dramatists. Aristotle's historical notes became recipes for success.

un événement véritable pour sujet."[10] All seventeenth-century dramatists seem to have heeded this lesson and, as Gustave Lanson points out, only Du Ryer's *Alcionée* and Rotrou's *Venceslas* escaped the general trends.[11]

Aristotle noted that the best tragedies were not simple, but rather that they contained sudden changes of fortune. Modern critics were unable to disagree, for "la tragédie simple, au sens d'Aristote, sans péripétie ni reconnaissance, est inconnue au XVIIᵉ siècle."[12] They did, however, insist on the unity of action, and Chapelain, in his *Lettre sur les 24 heures*, voiced the general opinion when he stated: "Je nie que le meilleur poème dramatique soit celui qui embrasse le plus d'actions, et dis au contraire qu'il n'en doit contenir qu'une et qu'il ne la faut encore que de bien médiocre longueur."[13] Racine made this rule his very own when he stated, in the preface to *Bérénice*, that "il n'y a que le vraisemblable qui touche dans la tragédie; et quelle vraisemblance y a-t-il qu'il arrive en un jour une multitude de choses qui pourraient à peine arriver en plusieurs semaines?" But, while Racine, in this respect, agreed with the critics that preceded him, many of his fellow dramatists did not, and as he suggested in his preface to *Bérénice*, "l'Œdipe même, quoique tout plein de reconnaissances, est moins chargé de matière que la plus simple tragédie de nos jours. . . . Il y en a qui pensent que cette simplicité est une marque de peu d'invention. Ils ne songent pas qu'au contraire toute l'invention consiste à faire quelque chose de rien." Most of these critics were obscure poetasters, but even Corneille opposed him on that score, and it was for Corneille that this passage of the first preface to *Britannicus* was intended: to satisfy these critics, "Il ne faudrait que s'écarter du

10. Alfred C. Hunter (ed.), *Jean Chapelain: Opuscules critiques* (Paris: Droz, 1936), pp. 119-20.
11. *Esquisse d'une histoire de la tragédie en France* (New York: Columbia University Press, 1921), p. 73.
12. Bray, p. 311.
13. Hunter, p. 120.

4

naturel pour se jeter dans l'extraordinaire. Au lieu d'une action simple, chargée de peu de matière, telle que doit être une action qui se passe en un seul jour, et qui, s'avançant par degrés vers sa fin, n'est soutenue que par les intérêts, les sentiments et les passions des personnages, il faudrait remplir cette même action de quantité d'incidents qui ne se pourraient passer qu'en un mois, d'un grand nombre de jeux de théâtre d'autant plus surprenants qu'ils seraient moins vraisemblables, d'une infinité de déclamations où l'on ferait dire aux acteurs tout le contraire de ce qu'ils devraient dire."

Must we then resign ourselves to see disagreement on this score among the major dramatists of the century? No, for, as Saint-Evremond pointed out in the third part of his defense of Corneille, the latter's work marks a stage on the road to perfect unity of action. Corneille "tenait trop aux sujets pour les sacrifier aux caractères."[14] As time went on, the public of the seventeenth century shifted its favor from the former to the latter, and Saint-Évremond, in 1677, said with nostalgia that "il y a eu des temps où il falloit choisir de beaux sujets, et les bien traiter: il ne faut plus aujourd'hui que des caractères."[15]

While there was a tendency to agree on the first point, there was much dissension on the second, that of characters or, as La Mesnardière interpreted the word, "les mœurs." According to Aristotle, since the very aim of tragedy is to evoke fear and pity, the hero must be chosen to bring about this end. He cannot be wholly good or wholly bad. He must have a flaw and succumb to misfortune because of that flaw, thus evoking pity without outright indignation. Racine, in the preface to *Iphigénie en Aulide*, pointed out that the very presence of Eriphile was dictated by this thought: "Quelle apparence que j'eusse souillé la scène par le meurtre horrible

14. Bray, p. 314.
15. *Œuvres mêlées* (Paris: Techener, 1865), II, 415.

d'une personne aussi vertueuse et aussi aimable qu'il fallait
représenter Iphigénie?" Chapelain, and most French critics
for that matter, accepted this definition of the tragic heroes
"dont les fins ont été malheureuses et qui n'étaient ni trop
bons ni trop méchants."[16] Others—Vossius, Le Bossu, and La
Mesnardière in France, Castelvetro among others in Italy—
disagreed, readily visualizing a virtuous hero such as Ulysses
or a truly evil one such as Medea. La Mesnardière, however,
cautioned against the dangers of such a choice which could
only be "nuisible." Corneille, with Polyeucte, put a saint on
stage, and, with Médée and Cléopatre, the "second Medea,"
two truly evil characters. As we shall see later, when we take
a closer look at the tragic hero, Corneille's hero is perhaps
furthest removed in his very essence from the Aristotelian
hero. There is, however, one aspect of this problem which
needs to be discussed here: "Mais le héros n'est pas seul dans
la tragédie, il lui faut au moins un antagoniste. Ici nous en-
trons dans la théorie des cas tragiques."[17] Aristotle had vis-
ualized four such situations: the conscious murder of a friend
or of a relative; the recognition—as a friend or relative—of
a person who has just been murdered; a murder prevented
by the recognition; a projected murder of a relative which is
rejected. Aristotle rejected the last entirely as theatrically
bad; he considered the first too odious to be very good; the
second, while better, he felt to be still inferior to the third,
the best of all. Most critics agreed, but again Corneille did
not. He considered the third case the worst of all, preferring
by far the fourth. It is easy to see that this preference found
its application in such masterpieces as *Le Cid*, *Cinna*, and
Nicomède. As Gustave Lanson suggests, it is precisely in this
aspect that Corneille is least "Aristotelian," since Aristotle
seemed to prefer recognition scenes while Corneille's heroes

16. Hunter, p. 130.
17. Bray, p. 316.

are always aware of the path that they take and of its dangers.[18]

It is in the treatment of passions that the greatest gulf exists between Greek and French tragedy. Aristotle mentioned that the passions depicted on stage should evoke terror and pity. Laudun went still further and insisted on the predominance of cruelty, and most of the critics at the very beginning of the seventeenth century translated Aristotle's key word not as *terror*, but as *horror*. This is in part explained by R. C. Knight when he states that "Seneca writes tragedy as if he had never heard of the *Poetics*—as perhaps he had not. And it is Seneca, because his elegant Latin was so much more attractive than the difficult Greek of his betters, who shaped and spoilt the tragedy of the French Renaissance."[19] The *Poetics* may have been the *livre de chevet* of most critics of the day, but the heritage of the sixteenth century could not be denied. As of 1639, however, La Mesnardière pointed out the fallacy: terror and not horror is a tragic passion. However, even this toning down was considered too little by the majority of the mid-century critics and dramatists. Mairet, in the preface to *La Sophonisbe* (1635), La Mesnardière four years later, d'Aubignac in his *Troisième dissertation* (1663), all suggested that pity must take precedence over fear, and Racine, in the preface to *Bérénice* (1670), settled the matter when he stated: "Ce n'est point une nécessité qu'il y ait du sang et des morts dans une tragédie: il suffit que l'action en soit grande, que les acteurs en soient héroïques, que les passions y soient excitées, et que tout s'y ressente de cette tristesse majestueuse qui fait tout le plaisir de la tragédie." But Racine went further: in the heart of the spectator, pity, evoked by love, displaced fear. Love thus became *the* passion,

18. *Corneille* (Paris: Hachette, 1898), p. 70.
19. "A Minimal Definition of Seventeenth-Century Tragedy," *FS* 10 (1956), 298.

7

and it is in this manner that Racine is furthest removed from the Greek.

Corneille too deviated from the Greek concept of the passions of tragedy, but in an even more radical manner, for he rejected the very idea of pity: in his preface to *Nicomède*, he suggested that his play was "extraordinaire" in that in it "la tendresse et les passions, qui doivent être l'âme des tragédies, n'ont aucune part en celle-ci; la grandeur de courage y règne seule, et regarde son malheur d'un œil si dédaigneux qu'il n'en saurait arracher une plainte." Corneille readily admitted that his hero "ne cherche point à faire pitié," and defended this position: "Dans l'admiration qu'on a pour sa vertu, je trouve une manière de purger les passions, dont n'a point parlé Aristote, et qui est peut-être plus sûre que celle qu'il prescrit à la tragédie par le moyen de la pitié et de la crainte." And so, as René Bray has pointed out, French tragedy, while seeming to accept Aristotle's precepts, really "renverse l'échelle des cas tragiques" that he had established. Corneille opted for a "pathétique d'admiration," while Racine and the rest of the dramatists of the century made love the prime "ressort."[20] As we shall soon see, Tristan's tragic world rejected the "pathétique d'admiration," and, while seeming, in many instances, to point to Racine, failed to abandon the purely pathetic situation for a profound psychological analysis of love the passion.

In the words of R. C. Knight, "I would propose to see the common seventeenth-century Tragedy in the first place as a Form, which is a species of the genus Drama, subject therefore to such requirements as *vraisemblance* and *bienséance*, which are laws of Drama, and distinguished from Comedy still by the four points of Lanson, modified in only one particular: *historique ou légendaire, royale, élevée de style*, and if not *sanglante* of necessity . . . at least including that Peril

20. Bray, pp. 321-22.

on which Corneille founds his Unity of Action" (p. 305).
This definition fits all dramatists, Corneille as well as Racine,
Tristan as well as La Serre. But it is a limited definition, one
concerned only with forms, with an artificial genre, tragedy.
Unfortunately, there can be no such vast and all-engulfing
definition of "tragic," for while tragedy defines a structure
—and how can a structure or a form be tragic?—"le tragique . . . est une dimension de l'existence réelle. La tragédie
est de l'ordre de la littérature et du théâtre, mais le tragique
est de l'ordre de la vie."[21]

21. Henri Gouhier, "Tragique et transcendance," in *Le théâtre tragique*,
ed. Jean Jacquot (Paris: CNRS, 1962), p. 479.

1. THE TRAGIC HERO
A MINIMAL DEFINITION

If one attempts a definition of the tragic hero, one finds the same problem as that presented in the previous chapter: to the extent that the hero belongs to the form, he is readily definable—a noble man occupied by noble deeds and coping with what might be loosely called his destiny—but beyond that, when he and his audience are on the threshold of "l'existence réelle," the archetype disappears. Are we in fact, at that moment, dealing with a character, with what the French call a *personnage?* In *Die Geburt der Tragödie*, Nietzsche suggested that "alle Individuen als Individuen komisch und damit untragisch seien: woraus zu entnehmen wäre, dass die Griechen überhaupt Individuen auf der tragischen Bühne nicht ertragen *konnten*. In der Tat scheinen sie so empfunden zu haben."[1]

What then is the tragic hero? Again, a brief look at his Hellenistic ancestor will help us in our search: "Es ist eine unanfechtbare Überlieferung, dass die Griechische Tragödie in ihrer ältesten Gestalt nur die Leiden Dionysus zum Gegenstand hatte, und dass der längere Zeit hindurch einzig vorhandene Bühnenheld eben Dionysus war. Aber mit der gleichen Sicherheit darf behauptet werden, dass niemals bis auf Euripides Dionysus aufgehört hat, der tragische Held zu sein, sondern dass alle die berühmten Figuren der griechischen Bühne, Prometheus, Ödipus usw. nur Masken jenes ursprünglichen Helden Dionysus sind" (*ibid.*) With Euripides, we enter into a new world. Dionysus was replaced, but not the idea of an ideal. It was due to the fact that the

1. *Werke* (München: Hanser, 1954), I, 61.

10

god hid behind these masks that the characters were able to assume the *Idealität* that the Greeks so admired. As Euripides changed the ideal, so did the French of the seventeenth century, and within that century, different authors beheld that ideal each in his own way. These *aperçus*, being basic and coming from the authors' very psychological nature, vary from one author to another, but are constant within each man's work. Corneille and Racine mature, and this is shown in their life's work; but they basically remain true to themselves, and this shows too.

Both Corneille and Racine deal with a world in which the prime *ressort* is the pursuit of a hidden reality. Whence the tragic? "En raison du caractère exorbitant de son ambition, la poursuite du caché s'expose à l'échec et à la déception."[2] Here, a parenthesis is needed, for the key word in our next point is the French word *regard*, and the dictionaries are of little or no help in defining it. Larousse merely suggests "action ou manière de regarder" and, for *regarder*, "jeter la vue sur." Littré gets us no further, and Mansion gives, as English equivalents, "look, glance, gaze." But none of these suffice. The *regard* goes far beyond the initial contact with the object under consideration. Faced with Poppaea's veil, with hidden beauty, with any mystery, it becomes a perseverant quest for something that may well escape forever. As Goethe suggests in the *Römische Elegien*, "Sehe mit fühlendem Aug'," the *regard*, at the risk of losing its own nature, wishes to touch, to grasp that which flees. It does not merely wish to "recueillir des images," but tries desperately to "établir une relation."[3] Man seeking the truth beyond the veil is called to action, but if, by chance or by perseverance he should glance upon the true nature of things, and should he understand, he will cease to act: "Die Erkenntnis tötet das

---

2. Jean Starobinski, *L'œil vivant* (Paris: Gallimard, 1961), p. 16.
3. *Ibid.*, p. 13.

Handeln, zum Handeln gehört das Umschleiertsein durch die Illusion—das ist die Hamletlehre. . . . In der Bewusstheit der einmal geschauten Wahrheit sieht jetzt der Mensch überall nur das Entsetzliche oder Absurde des Seins, jetzt versteht er das Symbolische im Schicksal der Ophelia, jetzt erkennt er die Weisheit des Walgottes Silen: es ekelt ihn."[4]

The dangers involved in *regarder* have always fascinated writers all over the world—Orpheus, Narcissus, Oedipus, Psyche, Medusa, even King David and Bluebeard are known to all—and the potential of this basic problem did not escape the best dramatists of seventeenth-century France.

"Chez Corneille, tout commence par l'éblouissement."[5] The drama of *Le Cid* does not really begin until Don Diègue asks the famous question, "Rodrigue, as-tu du cœur?" In the very first scene of *Mélite*, Tircis sees a lovely face and forgets everything else. Dorante, in *Le menteur*, is *ébloui* by "le tout Paris," and in *La suite du menteur*, by a mere portrait. In *La toison d'or*, such a portrait manages to change an entire stage into a resplendent garden. This is not solely Corneille's concept. As Professor Starobinski has pointed out, it is the leitmotiv of the *Guirlande de Julie*, of all the poems on the theme of the "Belle matineuse," and many others (p. 32). This *éblouissement*, it goes without saying, is an all-devouring and consuming light. To wrench himself free, the Cornelian hero must regain his cognizant state. By a willful act, he must not only destroy his momentary blindness, but become *éblouissant* himself.

When young Rodrigue is faced with his father's question, when he is *ébloui*, there is no hesitation: "Tout autre que mon père/ L'éprouverait sur l'heure." Is he at that moment truly *éblouissant?* No; rather, he is imbued with a will to be. He has donned a mask; he has set out to fulfill his own destiny

4. Nietzsche, p. 48.
5. Starobinski, p. 18.

and is condemned to strive to become that which, at that creative moment, he claims to be.[6]

We have suggested that, in Corneille's works, both the comic and the tragic hero are merely appearing; for the tragic hero, this appearance is neither an image of a pre-existing fact, nor an out-and-out lie. "Whether kings or less than kings, Corneille's heroes owe their sense of self to the *maison* of which they were born (or, in the case of certain problematic heroes, to their sense of how those so born should behave). . . . In the greater number of plays, by far, the Cornelian *généreux* is noble and virtuous (Latin: virtus, manly as well as morally pure) in birth and in station and *thus* noble and virtuous in deed. His duty may, as Nadal and others have stressed, be to himself, but his sense of self is derived, not forged. . . . The ethos is 'essentialist' rather than 'existentialist.' "[7] Rodrique dons a mask, he plays a role, but it is an essential role—if such a contradiction in terms can be forgiven—that is to say that the role he plays is in the fulfillment of his destiny. He strives to become the mask, a mask that is nothing more than the realization of his capabilities. As Théophile de Viau puts it, "Tout homme de courage est maître de son sort."[8] Dorante, on the other hand, dons a mask that has no connection with his essence. When his father asks "Etes-vous gentilhomme?" (line 1501), it is precisely because the son has lied: "Qui se dit gentilhomme, et ment comme tu fais,/ Il ment quand il le dit, et ne le fut jamais" (lines 1519-20). From the very moment of *éblouisse-*

6. If *Le Cid* lacks unity, it is not because of the presence of the Infante, but because there are three basic *éblouissements*, each marking the beginning of a quest. We have already mentioned the first; the second begins when Rodrigue realizes that he must fill the shoes of the man he has killed; the third, that of Chimène, is doomed to frustration in spite of the final words of the king.

7. Robert J. Nelson, *Corneille. His Heroes and Their Worlds* (Philadelphia: University of Pennsylvania Press, 1963), pp. 20-21.

8. *Pyrame et Thisbé*, III, 2. It is important to remember that *courage* and *cœur* were synonyms at that time.

13

ment, the Cornelian hero must, by his deeds, prove that his boast was not empty. He must become what he has claimed to be. The essential hero can either succeed (Rodrigue) or fail due to circumstances beyond his control (Chimène). The comic anti-hero, who has assumed a non-essential role and therefore plays with social—relative—values, is doomed to be ridiculous. Thus, the Cornelian tragic hero knows that the world's eyes are on him, and he thirsts for this condition. His sacrifices (be it of his life or of his beloved) are valid only insofar as they are public, "car le moi n'existe pleinement que s'il est *apparaissant*."[9]

Racine's tragic hero, like Corneille's, feels an eye upon him. Unlike Corneille's hero, he cannot escape that *regard* which fills him with shame and guilt. Corneille permits his heroes to go beyond the tragic moment; in that author's words, they want to "ravir d'admiration." Racine like Shakespeare, sees the true grandeur of tragedy in the fact that it puts before our eyes the full horror of human suffering, a horror that brings about terror and pity. Shakespeare and Racine are not dealing with man as he should be, but as he is, and, as a result, can go to the very limit of human suffering. In Corneille, we may see death without suffering. Yet, what is more pathetic than Lear's "O, let me not be mad, not mad, sweet heaven!" (I.v) or Bérénice's "Je vivrai, je suivrai vos ordres absolus./ Adieu, seigneur, régnez: je ne vous verrai plus" (1493-94).

While Corneille's theater is full of movement and gestures, that of Racine is remarkably static. "Les scènes, chez Racine, sont des *entrevues*"[10] in which the protagonists exchange *regards*. A gesture is physical; a searching look, however full of physical implications it may be, transcends the corporeal —and thus the need for physical violence—to search the very soul of the protagonist. Is it then surprising if the protagonist,

9. Starobinski, p. 72.   10. *Ibid.*, p. 74.

wishing to escape this searching, judging look, breaks the spell, if only to bring about complete disaster? The eyes, then, are more than the "miroirs de l'âme" of the *précieux;* they are the very doors to the deepest and most rigorous of soul-searchings. Théramène tells Hippolyte as much in the first scene of *Phèdre:* "Chargés d'un feu secret, vos yeux s'appesantissent" (134). Two scenes later, Phèdre herself feels it:

> Œnone, la rougeur me couvre le visage:
> Je te laisse trop voir mes honteuses douleurs,
> Et mes yeux, malgré moi, se remplissent de pleurs.
>
> (182-84)

She will continue to feel judged until the very end, for if the eyes are the means by which we see, they also make us aware of the fact that we are seen:

> Déjà je ne vois plus qu'à travers un nuage
> Et le ciel et l'époux que ma présence outrage;
> Et la mort, à mes yeux dérobant la clarté,
> Rend au jour, qu'ils souillaient, toute sa pureté.
>
> (1641-44)

This is because "le regard n'est point tourné vers des objets. . . . Il n'explore pas le monde, interroge à peine la nature: il ne cherche que le regard des autres . . . il n'est préoccupé que d'avoir prise sur quelqu'un, et de savoir si les yeux qu'il cherche le regardent ou l'ignorent en retour."[11] Is there a more Racinian line than Phèdre's "Je le vis, je rougis, je pâlis à sa vue" (173)?

From the moment he sees that he is seen, with that vision the Racinian hero becomes aware of his destiny, for it is invariably a nefarious vision, a forbidden one: Roxane should not have seen Bajazet, Phèdre should not have seen Hippo-

11. *Ibid.,* p. 77.

15

lyte. The *regard* becomes thirst, a thirst that cannot be quenched. It is then just a matter of time before the frustration becomes a destructive rage. It is at that moment that the *voyeur* becomes executioner; it is then that he feels the bitterness of his sorrow, the depth of his misery. From guilt to rage —a sadistic rage heightened by the provocative glance of the victim—and on to a greater guilt, that is the road that all Racinian heroes must travel.

It would be wrong to consider this "poétique du regard" a Racinian monopoly. We will see that Tristan had already tried in his earliest plays, as did a contemporary of Tristan, La Serre. In *Thomas Morus* (1642), the clash between Thomas More and Henry VIII is set aside early in the play to make way for a more popular one, the love affair between Henry VIII and Anne Boleyn (Arténice): "Vos larmes me brûlent aussi bien que vos regards" (I.iv), admits a king who can no longer be a good ruler: "Dès que l'Amour me banda les yeux il m'arracha la Couronne" (III.ii). By the same token, in Du Ryer's *Alcionée* (1637) the dialogues between Lydie and Alcionée are veritable duels in which the would-be lovers, trying to exchange *regards* which can only fail to grasp the hidden vision, vie in cruelty. "Voulez-vous plaire enfin, à mon œil offensé?" is the question asked by Lydie (873). When Alcionée fulfills her apparent wish,

> Vous m'aviez commandé de vivre, et j'ai vécu,
> Vous m'aviez commandé de vaincre, et j'ai vaincu,
> Aujourd'hui vos rigueurs ont demandé ma vie,
> Mon bras obéissant la donne à votre envie,   (1585-88)

she finally *sees* his innocence in his eyes, "Ses yeux déjà tournés vers la mortelle barque" (1559), but it is too late: recognizing in herself her lover's executioner ("j'impose à ma rigueur le crime de ton bras" [1682]), she can only determine her own punishment. Unfortunately, Du Ryer's heroine remains romanesque at a moment when, in Racine's hand, she would have been tragic. Her decision, "Que pour mon châtiment je t'aime après ta mort" (1686), is, at best, ludicrous in view of the enormity of her fault. Phèdre and Hermione, Hérode and La Fille du Mouphti are of another caliber.

As has been stated above, the Racinian *regard* is a desire to see all, to grasp all, in one word, to be all. But, in this world of relative values, that is impossible. As Pascal put it, add something finite to something finite, and you still haven't changed it in relation to the infinite. With his desire for the absolute, the tragic hero faces a world of relative values and finds that, as a result, "le conflit entre le héros et le monde est radical et insoluble."[12] This is accentuated by the fact that this world has rules and laws which force us to make constant choices. We are constantly asked to sacrifice in order to achieve, but the Racinian hero "demande le refus de tout compromis, de tout choix, parce que pour lui le choix constitue *le* mal, *le* péché par excellence."[13] In this tragic situation, the hero is confronted with two *présences:* a world that lacks values and is omnipresent, and a God, "la seule valeur authentique, mais qui reste toujours muet."[14] Between these two stands man in all his Pascalian grandeur and misery, aware of this value, yet unable to realize it. But, and therein lies his grandeur, the tragic hero finds greatness precisely at the moment of doom. As Pascal stated, "quand même l'univers l'écraserait, l'homme serait encore plus noble que ce qui le tue, parce qu'il sait qu'il meurt, et l'avantage que l'univers a sur lui; l'univers n'en sait rien."[15]

How does the tragic hero face this problem? There can be only one valid answer, a systematic and total rejection of the world and of life. Most of Racine's heroes see this, but they

12. Lucien Goldmann, "Structure de la tragédie racinienne," in *Le théâtre tragique*, p. 254.
13. *Ibid.*, p. 255.   14. *Ibid.*, p. 256.   15. *Pensée* 347.

17

are loath to do so, and it usually takes five acts for them to reconcile themselves to the idea. Thus, Phèdre, who at the very beginning declares "Soleil, je te viens voir pour la dernière fois" (172), is still in—or rather, has returned to—that position at the end of the play:

> Déjà je ne vois plus qu'à travers un nuage
> Et le ciel et l'époux que ma présence outrage;
> Et la mort, à mes yeux dérobant la clarté,
> Rend au jour, qu'ils souillaient, toute sa pureté.
>
> (1641-44)

Even in *Bérénice*, this separation from the world is not manifest until the end, when Antiochus' "Hélas!" coming on the heels of Bérénice's "Pour la dernière fois, adieu, seigneur," shows how far above the world (Antiochus) is the tragic universe (Titus and Bérénice).

If Racine's drama is one of perdition, if his heroes reject this world, it is precisely because they have accepted its values. Many of Tristan's heroes, on the contrary, reject these values. Their destiny is one which, while imposed on them, does not triumph over their will. It may crush them, but even as it does, it cannot break down the walls that these heroes have built around themselves. Here again, one may find Pascal's *pensée 347* very apt, for at the moment of his death, the hero knows why he dies, but the executioner does not, or, as in the case of Camus' *L'Etranger*, thinks of false reasons.[16]

Daniella Dalla Valle, in her monumental thesis on the theater of Tristan,[17] suggests that the poet, rather than the dramatist, feels the solitude, the inability—or unwillingness —to communicate which separates him from his world. Thus

16. As Meursault makes clear in the penultimate paragraph of *L'Etranger*, he is being executed, not for the murder of an Arab, but "pour n'avoir pas pleuré à l'enterrement de ma mère."

17. *Il teatro di Tristan l'Hermite* (Torino: Giappichelli, 1964), p. 293.

18

Tristan, seldom great dramatist but always good poet, presents heroes unable or unwilling to communicate with one another, and it is this isolation which is the basis of their tragic situation. Hérode loves Mariane and cannot understand her hatred; he is ready to forgive her for what he believes is an attempt on his life, but he cannot overlook his belief in her infidelity, and it is this alleged crime that leads to her execution. Regicide or adultery—both crimes exist only in the mind of Hérode, and they exist there because Mariane has made all communication between them impossible.

This solitude is everywhere evident in Tristan's work and is even present in his comedy where it is transformed into a simple *quid pro quo:* "E quando degli stessi motivi egli ha osservato dall'esterno gli effetti comici, trasformando l'incomunicabilità in quiproquo, la solitudine in fissazione maniaca, l'ostentazione in smargiassata, e su questi temi ha orchestrato il suo gioco scenico, dimenticando l'angoscia nel riso, abbiamo avuto il terzo capolavoro: il *Parasite.*"[18] Miss Dalla Valle further suggests that most of Tristan's characters are baroque with certain existential tendencies. Such classifications are difficult not only to establish, but to maintain. There have always been Hamlets and Fausts, heroes simultaneously baroque, romantic, and existential. The baroque hero, like his romantic counterpart, is a rebel. He seeks, as does Molière's Sosie or Tristan's Ariste, to establish his own identity, to find out just what human nature is, and to determine his role in the world that surrounds him. He especially wants to find his authentic and dynamic *moi* in a world that is basically set. When this dynamic *moi* (the Sartrian *pour soi*) clashes with set conformity (the *en soi*), anguish must result, for the hero, be he baroque or existential, can no longer reconcile his *ser* with the *estar* of the world. While every hero will

18. *Ibid.*

19

protest, only the romantic will try suicide: not only is the baroque hero too religious to kill himself, but his awareness of the absurd is too necessary to allow him the luxury of suicide.[19]

One more general point must be discussed here. While Racine's heroes are always conscious of the importance of their deeds, those of Tristan, isolated, are not. "Nella tragedia classica i protagonisti hanno coscienza degli ostacoli che incontrano sul loro cammino."[20] This is what Schérer points out when he sees, as the basis of the dilemma, an impossible choice between "deux attitudes également légitimes, mais inconciliables. . . . Prenant conscience de cette situation, le héros l'exprimera en un raisonnement qui pèse tour à tour chacune des deux possibilités, montre que la réalisation de chacune d'elles conduit à l'inacceptable sacrifice de l'autre et qu'il est par suite incapable de réaliser aucune des deux."[21] But if the Racinian heroes succumb to their passions in spite of their awareness, Hérode, Fauste, Panthée, la Fille du Mouphti see the consequences of their acts only when it is too late: "In Tristan, invece, il dilemma non esiste: lo scioglimento tragico trae, sì, le sue origini da un fattore umano, ma l'eroe si rende conto della propria responsabilità soltanto quando gli eventi stanno precipitando (la fille du Mouphti in *Osman*) o quando la catastrofe ha già avuto luogo (Hérode nella *Mariane*, Fauste nella *Mort de Chrispe*, Panthée nella tragedia omonima). Gli eroi di Tristan, cioè, non sono mai tanto lucidi da concepire l'esistenza di due soluzioni e da saperne prevedere e soppesare gli sviluppi e le conseguenze. . . . Solo Ariste, il personaggio meditativo per eccellenza del teatro di Tristan, di fronte alla sventura che lo colpisce, giunge a prendere coscienza di due possibili reazioni e, conseguentemente, cade nel dubbio; ed è il dubbio esisten-

19. Sénèque and Fauste, in committing suicide, only follow royal edicts.
20. Dalla Valle, p. 121.
21. *La dramaturgie classique*, p. 67.

ziale nella sua forma estrema, il dubbio vita o morte, essere o
non essere (vv. 165-204, pp. 18-19), dubbio che resta irri-
solto e porta alla follia."[22]

This personal meditation of Ariste "nasce di fronte ai colpi
del destino (in questo caso l'inattesa prepotenza del re), che
fanno sentire l'uomo inerme ed indifeso."[23] This omnipotent
and omnipresent destiny is also noted by Hérode: "Ce
qu'écrit le destin ne peut être effacé" (146). When confronted with this incomprehensible force, the hero of Tristan
will consult nature (*Panthée*, 341) or God (*Folie du sage*,
189-92) but invariably, when he fails to get an answer
from either, he will divorce himself from the values of that
absurd world. Andromaque survives in a world in which
her foes succumb to their passions; Mariane, willful architect
of her own destiny, succumbs because of her intransigence,
and proud among foes who feel their inferiority, goes to her
doom, dragging with her those whose values she has rejected.[24]

22. Dalla Valle, pp. 121-22.
23. *Ibid.*, p. 139.
24. The preceding two paragraphs have been abstracted from an introduction, written by J. W. Schweitzer and myself, to a forthcoming edition
of the theater of Tristan.

2. THE ESSENTIAL STRANGER

While the main subject of *La Mariane* is well known, it might be well to review rapidly those details emphasized by Tristan in his version of the tragedy. Hérode, having crushed the power of the Hasmonaean dynasty, solidifies his position on the throne of Judea by forcing Mariane, a princess of the Hasmonaean line, to marry him. Although she bears him several children, Mariane's pride prevents her from truly loving Hérode, while it antagonizes Hérode's siblings, Salomé and Phérore. Hérode having killed her father and brother, Mariane's feelings turn to hatred. When she finds out that Hérode, upon leaving for Rhodes, left orders that she be killed should he die, her rage knows no bounds. Henceforth she will have nothing more to do with her husband. A gesture dictated by ferocious jealousy becomes, in Mariane's eyes, "una prova del non amore del marito."[1] The murder of Aristobule and the near-murder of Mariane separate the husband and wife, and every time that Hérode will seek to speak with Mariane, he will be confronted—as he is in the first scene of the play—by the ghost of the slain Hasmonaean.

If *La Mariane* is Tristan's masterpiece, it is so because "il suo nucleo si colloca pressochè interamente in quella zona di solitudine e ostentazione, di sofferta incomunicabilità,"[2] a solitude sought and enforced by Mariane's essential pride. From the opening line, we see a Hérode alone with his dreams, boisterously confident,

> Et j'ai trop sûrement affermi mon Empire
> Pour craindre les malheurs que tu me viens prédire,

> (7-8)

1. Dalla Valle, p. 228.
2. *Ibid.*

22

yet longing to communicate with someone. Lacy Lockert, analyzing the play, claims that "Herod and not its titular heroine is the central character in his *Mariamne* [*sic*]. The entire play is built around him, to exhibit the uncontrolled, furious, warring passions that possess him and sweep him on to the judicial murder of the woman who is their object, and his subsequent paroxysms of remorse."[3] While it is quite true that the role of Hérode is by far the most demanding, the above statement seems to be an oversimplification of a great poetic situation. Miss Dalla Valle is far more convincing when she suggests that "Hérode esiste poeticamente in quanto ama e non è amato, dice il suo amore e non è creduto, chiede di essere illuso ed è disilluso. E Mariane esiste poeticamente solo in ragione del suo odio incompreso e non corrisposto, cui Hérode offre in cambio un amore cui lei non crede e che lei non vuole. Hérode e Mariane sono, quindi, poeticamente uniti fin da queste prime apparizioni in cui non s'incontrano; essi formano un nodo indissolubile e si condizionano a vicenda."[4] Hérode and Mariane cannot exist one without the other and the tragedy exists primarily because Mariane, failing to realize that Hérode is as necessary to her hatred as she is to his love, rejects all his overtures. Like Corneille's Médée, out of place in Jason's world, she mistakes her moral superiority for a limitless self-sufficiency which exists only in her mind, for her hatred is essential to her identity, and it cannot exist in a vacuum.

Even though Mariane does not appear in person until the second act, she is omnipresent in the first. Hérode, relating his dream, gives us the first clue:

Je me suis trouvé seul dans un bois écarté,
Où l'horreur habitait avec l'obscurité,
Lorsqu'une voix plaintive a percé les ténèbres,

3. *Studies in French Classical Tragedy* (Nashville: Vanderbilt University Press, 1958), pp. 119-20.   4. Pages 230-31.

23

> Appelant Mariane, avec des tons funèbres.
> J'ai couru vers le lieu d'où le bruit s'épandait,
> Suivant dans ce transport l'Amour qui me guidait,
> Et qui semblait encor m'avoir prêté ses ailes,
> Pour atteindre plus tôt ce miracle des belles:
> Mes pas m'ont amené sur le bord d'un étang,
> Dont j'ai trouvé les eaux toutes rouges de sang;
> Il est tombé dessus un éclat de tonnerre;
> J'ai senti sous mes pieds un tremblement de terre,
> Et dessus ce rivage, environné d'effroi,
> Le jeune Aristobule a paru devant moi.   (93-106)

Whenever he seeks Mariane, he will find only the specter of the murdered Hasmonaeans, for she is

> Un cœur que je ne puis ranger sous mon pouvoir
> En possédant le corps où je le sens mouvoir. (217-18)

Why, cries he, must it be "Que son cœur soit de glace, et le mien soit de feu?" (238). To make matters worse, this rebuffed husband is, to use Mariane's word, a usurper who cannot but resent his wife's "humeur hautaine" (282). Moreover, this wife who embodies "Tout ce que la nature a fait pour me tenter" (274) is also the woman without whose help Hérode would have lost "à la fois, et le Sceptre, et le jour" (286).

Hérode only too readily forgives what his siblings cannot endure:

> Et puis, il est bien juste, à dire vérité,
> Qu'elle garde entre vous un peu de majesté.
> Mille rois glorieux sont ses dignes ancêtres,
> Et l'on peut la nommer la fille de nos maîtres.
>
> (293-96)

As Salomé puts it, Mariane "Parle de nous comme de ses valets" (298).

Mariane's opening lines show her utter contempt and hatred: in her husband, she sees only "un monstre abomina-

ble,/ Qui du trépas des miens me paraît tout sanglant" (348-
50). When Dina, her lady-in-waiting, suggests more re-
straint, she can only think of her glorious birth, and adds,

Si mon corps est captif, mon âme ne l'est pas:
Je laisse la contrainte aux serviles personnes,
Je sors de trop d'aïeux qui portaient des couronnes,
Pour avoir la pensée, et le front différents,
Et devenir esclave en faveur des tyrans.
Qu'Hérode m'importune, ou d'amour, ou de haine,
On me verra toujours vivre et mourir en reine.

(362-68)

Proud vestige of a noble line, forced to live with a "parvenu,"
Mariane faces a loneliness all the more terrible in that she
cannot forget her father and brother:

Soit lors que je repose, ou soit lors que je veille,
Leur plainte à tous moments vient frapper mon oreille;
Ils s'offrent à toute heure à mes yeux éplorés,
Je les vois tous sanglants et tous défigurés,
Ils me viennent conter leurs tristes aventures,
Ils me viennent montrer leurs mortelles blessures,
Et me vont reprochant pour me combler d'ennuis,
Qu'avecque leur bourreau je dors toutes les nuits.

(383-90)

While her tirade (379-428) is less lyrical than Hérode's, it
is equally striking, Mariane's rage and despair mounting as
she recalls each detail of Hérode's crimes. Her hatred has
been nurtured for some time, yet one can sense it grow during the entire tirade, culminating in a paroxysm of fury:

Et puis qu'après cela je flatte l'inhumain
Qui ne vient que d'ôter la vie à mon germain?
Plutôt le feu me brûle, ou l'onde son contraire
Rende mon corps pareil à celui de mon frère.

(425-28)

25

Dina's suggestion that this happened long ago (429), and that "On prend beaucoup de soin pour vous en consoler" (442), even her assertion that the king loves Mariane, is a waste of time: Mariane neither can nor wants to believe in a love that invades and infringes upon a solitude so essential to her position. She will be a stranger at her own trial: "Crois tout ce que tu dis, et tout ce que tu penses" (980), for

> Mon esprit que le Sort afflige au dernier point,
> Souffre les trahisons, mais il n'en commet point.
>
> (813-14)

She goads her husband:

> J'ai mille trahisons, et mille cruautés,
> Le meurtre d'un Aïeul, l'assassinat d'un Frère,
>
> (818-19)

until, blinded by his ill-controlled rage, he blurts out words of hatred—a hatred he does not feel, but one which Mariane can readily understand and which she can believe. And so it is with ferocious glee that she welcomes his outburst:

> Poursuis, poursuis barbare, et sois inexorable,
> Tu me rends un devoir qui m'est fort agréable,
> Et ta haine obstinée à me priver du jour,
> M'oblige beaucoup plus que n'a fait ton amour.
> Ici ta passion répond à mon envie,
> Tu flattes mon désir en menaçant ma vie,
> Je dois bénir l'excès de ta sévérité,
> Car je vais de la mort à l'immortalité.
> Ma tête bondissant du coup que tu lui donnes,
> S'en va dedans le Ciel se charger de couronnes,
> Dont les riches brillants n'ont point de pesanteur,
> Et que ne peut ravir un lâche usurpateur.   (855-66)

This is the Hérode she understands. When a few moments

later he corrects himself and speaks of love, when speaking to Love, he begs,

> Fais-lui voir que je l'aime à l'égal de moi-même,
> Et s'il se peut encore, Amour, fais qu'elle m'aime,
> (891-92)

he not only reaches a truly poetic height, but in so doing, he causes the impenetrable wall of misunderstanding to reappear:

> On connaît à ce style, et doux, et décevant,
> Comme en l'art de trahir ton esprit est savant;
> C'est avec trop de soin m'ouvrir la sépulture:
> Pour me perdre il suffit d'une seule imposture.
> (917-20)

But it is in her last scenes that Mariane shows herself for what she is. Her *stances* (1239-72), a perfect vehicle for pathos, only emphasize the heroic nature of the victim. No longer is she the Andromaque who cannot forget that she is also a mother. Time after time, she convinces herself of the unyielding nature of her heart:

> Un absolu pouvoir rend mon corps prisonnier:
> Mais en quelque péril que le malheur m'engage,
> J'aurai cet avantage
> Que mon cœur pour le moins se rendra le dernier.

Steadfast in the face of death, she resolutely divorces herself from this world:

> Quelque horreur qu'en la mort on puisse reconnaître
> Elle n'a qu'à paraître,
> J'irai la recevoir d'un visage assuré.

> Il est temps désormais que le Ciel me sépare
> D'avecque ce barbare,
> Son humeur et la mienne ont trop peu de rapport.

27

Having done this, she turns her eyes to the next world:

> Auteur de l'univers, souveraine puissance,
> Qui depuis ma naissance
> M'as toujours envoyé des matières de pleurs,
> Mon âme se résigne à tes bontés divines,
> Au milieu des épines,
> Seigneur, fais-moi bientôt marcher dessus des fleurs.

Having rejected those around her, she is at peace with her-self. For the first time, she is truly self-sufficient, and the pity of the Capitaine des Gardes is *de trop:* "Cette compassion m'est fort peu nécessaire" (1315). Her mother's sorrow is equally superfluous:

> Je voudrais que son cœur pût borner sa tristesse,
> Et que pour mon sujet elle eût moins de tendresse.
>
> (1359-60)

When this mother, afraid for her own life, decides to "éviter l'orage" (1309) by disowning her daughter who is on her way to the scaffold,

> Achève tes destins, méchante et malheureuse,
> Cette mort pour ton crime est trop peu rigoureuse,
> . . . .
>
> Femme sans piété, nouvelle Danaïde,
> Inhumaine, traîtresse, assassine perfide,
> . . . .
>
> Je ne te connais point, tu ne viens pas de moi.
>
> (1379-90)

Mariane, understanding, and without anger, simply replies: "Vous vivrez innocente, et je mourrai coupable" (1392). The divorce is complete. Perfect stranger, she no longer needs anyone or anything, not even Meursault's desired "cris de haine."

Not until the creation of *Osman*, his last tragedy, will Tristan return to the examination of the truly essential stranger. According to history, Osman becomes sultan in 1618, when not yet fourteen years old. In spite of his youth, he is a fairly good ruler; victories over Poland and Venice consecrate his glory. Nevertheless, it is a short reign. In 1621, he has his brother strangled. A brutal winter causes a famine. Osman's severity vis-à-vis his janissaries, his constant wars, his attempts to levy an army in Asia, all these factors add to the general discontent. When he makes public his desire to go to Mecca, the janissaries fear that this departure is merely a ruse that might allow Osman to join his Egyptian troops, thus ending the janissaries' control of military affairs. They rebel and Osman, trying to escape, is captured and thrown in jail where, in spite of his tears, he is strangled. Tristan follows history fairly closely, changing only the circumstances surrounding Osman's death and enhancing the role of the daughter of the mufti: Tristan's hero is not strangled, but dies gloriously before the gates of his palace, and the rebellion is due in large part to the scorned woman.

Osman, more than any other play by Tristan, is the tragedy of man "solo e impotente di fronte al destino, solo e infelice di fronte agli uomini."[5] It has been noted that Osman's sister "is allowed to drop out of the play after having taken a somewhat important part at its opening; and we are not even told what is her fate!"[6] The same critic remarks that she "lacks personality." This is all very true, but not necessarily a weakness of the play. At no time does she commit herself to action; at no time does she affect the outcome of the plot. She is not a participant. In fact, she has no name, being referred to as "la Sultane Sœur." In the tragic world of Tristan, the gods are called upon, but they seldom answer. Fate is the

5. Dalla Valle, p. 263.
6. Lockert, p. 116.

ruler, and a fickle one: "O Fortune inconstante et de qui les caprices" (333) are the words of Osman's sister, and he will echo them in the last act: "O Fortune! Nimphe inconstante" (1236). The gods, then, do not answer, but they do grant one small favor to a chosen few, a terrible favor which only enhances their misery: a vision of the future. The Sultane Sœur, with her vision of things to come, is alone and impotent "di fronte al destino." Sole believer in the content of her dreams, she is alone and unhappy "di fronte agli uomini." In her we have—in embryonic form, to be sure—the two main themes of the play. Once they have been embodied in Osman and the Fille du Mouphti, our Ottoman Cassandra is no longer necessary and disappears.

Like Mariane, Osman is a stranger in his own land. Truly "généreux," he is surrounded by "des animaux abrutis" (123). Expecting to find brothers in battle, he finds "un Eunuque au lieu d'un Janissaire" (118). Instead of valor, he finds intrigue. Even in love he is deceived: having fallen in love with a portrait of the Fille du Mouphti, he sees her only to find that the portrait had deceived him: "En ce pinceau trompeur j'eus trop de confiance" (430). Ironically, Osman who will succumb because of his pride, objects to the equally proud Fille du Mouphti because "elle a plus d'orgueil vingt fois que de beauté" (435). One might then say that he is alone before men, but a close reading of the play shows that this is not so. Like Mariane he soon realizes that he has nothing in common with those who surround him. At first he decides to go to Egypt where there are still men who can fight as he does (141-48). When this avenue is cut off, he is alone, face to face with his destiny.

From the start the young sultan is aware of his station:

> Ne porterais-je enfin le titre d'Empereur,
> Que pour être conduit par la commune erreur?
>
> (159-60)

He knows how to use this power—"Il sait que ma colère est assez redoutable" (222)—and has full confidence in the results:

> Dis lui qu'il m'est aisé de calmer la tempête
> Qui bruit près du Sérail et gronde sur sa tête,
> Et que le seul péril dont il est menacé,
> Est à n'achever pas ce qu'il a commencé.
> Il n'a qu'à satisfaire à mon ardente envie,
> Pour assurer par là mon bonheur et sa vie. (305-10)

He also knows that he is alone. He had plans to go to Egypt with "le plus beau des Trésors/ Que jamais la nature ait produit sur ces bords" (175-76), but when the Fille du Mouphti fails to meet his expectations, he will go alone: "Je prendrai seul le soin de conserver ma Gloire" (929), and when he leaves, it will be in broad daylight, like a sultan (969-87). This loneliness is accentuated by the fact that, although his bravery is essential and hereditary—"l'honneur de nos aïeux/ Dont la grandeur encore éclate dans nos yeux" (986-87)—his sister does not share it, showing, as she does, a weakness "indigne de ta race" (1021). This loneliness, how-ever, is maintained by the sheer will of a man who refuses the many human contacts offered. The Fille du Mouphti is rejected. Like Hérode before her, she embodies "la passione amorosa infelice e non corrisposta."[7] Like him, she will un-leash the forces which will doom the person she loves. These forces, in the persons of the rebellious soldiers, seek only "un moment d'audience" (1118), but Osman, from the start, has doomed this attempt to failure:

> Qui vous fait assembler pour me donner conseil?
> L'ombre est-elle en état d'éclairer le Soleil? (1076-77)

His set of values never changes. When the scorned Fille du Mouphti challenges him:

7. Dalla Valle, p. 264.

31

> Tu vois quel est le sort que t'a fait ton caprice,
> Que me peux-tu répondre en ce funeste jour?

his answer shows no regret: "Que je trouve mes maux plus doux que ton amour" (1329-31). Willful to the end, he finds himself in a position not unlike that of Polyeucte in Act IV, scene 3, of Corneille's play: the passionate declaration of the jilted girl weakens his resolve, but cannot destroy his "vertu":

> C'est assez, c'est assez, n'en dis pas davantage!
> Un si tendre propos amollit mon courage.
> J'ai besoin qu'il soit ferme en l'état où je suis,
> Et ces traits de ton zèle augmentent mes ennuis.
>
> (1380-83)

His death assured—and accepted (1389)—he eixts like sultan: his honor intact and his isolation complete.

3. THE EXISTENTIAL STRANGER

Mariane and Osman, by their very origin, were strangers in the worlds that surrounded them. Both were, in the tradition of the century, young and attractive, noble and bold. "Le héros classique est jeune; il est beau, cela va sans dire . . . [et il] doit briller par son courage et par sa noblesse."[1] As Phèdre describes the Thésée of yesteryear, who is "Charmant, jeune, traînant tous les cœurs après soi," so are Mariane and Osman. So is Chrispe, Fauste's "Idole charmante," but he, like Sénèque and Epicaris, becomes a stranger.

Sénèque, having educated Néron and taught him "des Rois le glorieux métier" (179), finds that although "Le Soleil n'a point fait trois fois un lustre entier" (180), he is now lost in an unjust and irrational world from which he seeks only to escape. At first, he seeks only to be left alone:

> Laisse à ton serviteur plus de tranquillité,
>
> . . . .
>
> Permets qu'ayant servi sous un si digne Maître,
> J'aille me délasser en un séjour champêtre,
> Où, bien loin du murmure et de l'empressement,
> Je puisse entretenir mes livres doucement. (192-200)

When this fails, when Néron's blind passions no longer make this dream possible, when he realizes that

> On ne trouve ici bas que les lois tyranniques,
> D'où naissent des effets tragiques,
> Et les Monstres y sont au dessus des Héros;

1. Scherer, p. 21.

> La Vertu sous le joug y demeure asservie:
> L'Orgueil, l'Ambition, l'Avarice et l'Envie
>   Nous y troublent à tous propos,   (1435-40)

then Sénèque turns to the "Principe de tout être," for only "là-haut, dans l'état d'une meilleure vie/ On goûte un éternel repos" (1441-42). Mariane saw in death little more than a release. Sénèque sees more: to die is to be reborn:

> Voici ce que je t'offre, ô Dieu libérateur.
> Dieu, dont le nouveau bruit a mon âme ravie,
> Dieu, qui n'es rien qu'amour, esprit, lumière et vie,
> Dieu de l'homme de Tharse, où je mets mon espoir:
> Mon âme vient de toi, veuille la recevoir.   (1433-37)

Mariane isolated herself from a world that was not hers and died to escape its values. Sénèque isolates himself from a world that is no longer his and in death finds the values that he has always held dear. La Serre, in his tragedy, *Thomas Morus* (1642), had presented a hero who, like Sénèque, could no longer reconcile the voice of his conscience with the deeds of his king. When the King does "ce qui m'a plu," Thomas does "ce qui était juste" (V.viii), and goes to his death because, as he stated at the beginning of the play, "les maximes de ma conscience me seront toujours plus considérables que celles de l'Etat" (I.i). Thomas More, a tragic hero, remains true to his values, goes nobly to a tragic death. This is not quite the case of Sénèque. In fact, Sénèque is the only character in the play whose destiny is not tragic: "la sua morte, infatti, non è catastrofe, ma liberazione, adempimento di un desiderio a lungo represso."[2]

La mort de Sénèque has eleven characters, all fairly important, none thoroughly described. It represents a world which gains some of its originality because of the "côtoiement de personnages si différents de naissance et de caractère": on

2. Dalla Valle, p. 249.

the one hand, Néron and Sabine; on the other, the coura-
geous Sénèque and Epicaris; between these extremes "évo-
luent ces personnages simplement à la mesure de l'homme:
les conjurés Pison, Rufus, Sévinus et Lucain, tour à tour
faibles et courageux."[3]

"Teatro di situazione,"[4] the play allows the characters to
reveal themselves by their deeds. The world that these deeds
reveal is one where, in fact, words are all too often mean-
ingless. Néron points this out very early in the play when
he plots the demise of his former teacher:

> Mais pour le perdre mieux il faut le caresser.
> Il faut lui tendre un piège avec tant d'artifice
> Qu'on lui puisse imputer notre propre malice;
> D'un filet si subtil il faut l'envelopper
> Qu'il s'y perde lui-même en pensant échapper,
> Et que les gens de bien, déçus par l'apparence,
> En le voyant périr, blâment son imprudence.
>
> (128-34)

While Mariane simply shuts out Hérode, we are here confronted with a world in which some people make any communication impossible. Just as Sénèque finds himself en-
meshed in Néron's *artifice* and *malice,* so does Epicaris find
the other rebels unequal to their word. She once loved
Néron: "Je t'aimais autrefois" (1731), but that was before
he became a "Monstre abîmé dans le crime" (1743). When
Epicaris sees that Néron's vices have taken over, she begins
to hate him. Her one passion, henceforth, is an all-consuming
love of liberty, a love that erases all other considerations and
thus isolates her from her more human co-conspirators. If
Lucain is a traitor to the cause, "Ce trait fait assez voir qu'il
n'eut jamais mon cœur" (1698).

3. Carriat, "Le théâtre de Tristan L'Hermite," *Le Travailleur de la Creuse* (September 4, 1947).
4. Dalla Valle, p. 252.

Nor does Néron escape this curse of loneliness. Guided and goaded by his wife, he soon finds out that, like Camus' Caligula, he is alone. He too could say "Je n'ai pas pris la voie qu'il fallait, je n'aboutis à rien. Ma liberté n'est pas la bonne," as Caligula puts it in his last scene. Instead, he blames Sabine and chases her:

> Eloigne-toi d'ici, fuis promptement, Sabine,
> De peur que ma colère éclate à ta ruine.
> O Ciel! qui me veux mal et que je veux braver,
> Des pièges que tu tends on ne se peut sauver:
> Tu prépares pour moi quelque éclat de tonnerre,
> Mais avant, je perdrai la moitié de la Terre.
>
> (1862-67)

And so the play ends with Néron alone on stage, alone with his crime and his ill-concealed remorse, "solo di fronte al destino e di fronte a se stesso,"[5] alone, but, as the last line of the play indicates, undaunted.

Sénèque is more fortunate than Néron in that respect, for in death he not only finds peace, but also true love. Until he learns of Néron's order for his death, Sénèque has thought only of his own peace, reputation, and glory. Now, his thoughts turn to his faithful wife Pauline:

> Il te souviendra bien qu'avec assez d'estime
> J'ai vécu près de toi sans reproche et sans crime;
> Il te souviendra bien de ma constante foi,
> Et que prêt à partir je n'eus regret qu'à toi.
>
> (1559-62)

This mild and reticent tirade brings a quick rejoinder from Pauline:

> Moi, je m'en souviendrai? Je veux qu'on se souvienne
> Qu'il ne fut point d'amour comparable à la mienne:

5. *Ibid.*, p. 251.

En vous suivant partout je veux montrer à tous,
Si vous viviez en moi, que je vivais en vous.   (1563-66)

The mutual declarations of love and devotion become more
and more exalted until the scene reaches a poetic intensity
seldom found in the seventeenth century. Together, they
die praising their new-found God, this "Dieu qui n'es rien
qu'amour, esprit, lumière et vie" (1835). Néron, hearing of
this death, fully realizes the depth of his loneliness. He can
only shrug off Sabine's "Qu'as-tu donc?" (1845) and, alone,
face the furies already invading his mind:

Une Erinne infernale à mes yeux se présente;
Un Fantôme sanglant me presse et m'épouvante.
Ne vois-je pas venir des bourreaux inhumains
Qui tiennent des serpents et des fouets en leurs mains?
(1850-53)

Sénèque is never more sure of himself than he is at the moment of his death. Epicaris, "la populacière esclave" whose
"basse origine n'ôte rien à l'héroïne généreuse qu'elle demeure,"[6] is equally sure of herself. Like Rotrou's Syra, she
is only sorry that she has failed. Syra points this out with
pride; she had only one plan:

Je veux purger l'état de l'objet de ma haine,
Et tends à me venger plus qu'à ma sûreté.

When it fails, she offers no apology:

J'ai juré de périr ou voir régner mon fils,
Et si la liberté m'était encore offerte,
J'en emploîrais pour lui tout l'usage à ta perte.
Est-ce assez?[7]

Epicaris is equally brave: "Je ne trahirai point des cœurs si

6. Carriat, "Le théâtre de Tristan L'Hermite" (September 15, 1947)
7. Cosroès, III.i; V.ii.

37

généreux" (1705), she replies to a menacing Néron whose threats are in vain, for she is sure of herself: "Mais je mourrai cent fois avant que je les nomme" (1712). The lonely tyrant lacks even this comfort; his enemies are dead or doomed, yet he alone is unsure of even his own frame of mind:

> Je ne sais ce que j'ai.
> Tous mes sens sont troublés, et mon âme inquiète
> Ne peut plus se remettre en sa première assiette:
> Je brûle de colère et frissonne d'effroi;
> Je forcène, j'enrage, et je ne sais pourquoi. (1845-49)

With *La mort de Chrispe* (1644), Tristan will return to the idea so well put forth in *La Mariane*, of a tragedy centered around two characters who do not understand each other. Fauste, the wife of Constantin, loves her stepson Chrispe who, in turn, loves—and is loved by—Constance. The jealous Fauste decides to rid herself of her rival by sending her a pair of poisoned gloves, a plan that backfires when Chrispe smells the gloves and shares Constance's fate. Constantin, upon learning the truth, orders Fauste's death.

Creator of an isolation that takes shape under our very eyes, Chrispe is not to be compared to Mariane. She was a total stranger from the beginning. He becomes a stranger, and even then only insofar as the tragic situation is concerned. Mariane needed Hérode as much as Hérode needed her, but if Fauste needs Chrispe, the young prince, surrounded by friends and with a love of his own, does not need Fauste. He is not a total stranger, he simply will not allow Fauste to enter into his world. All her attempts to speak of her love will be rejected by a hero "che non può, non sa, non vuole capire."[8]

Fauste loves Chrispe, yet cannot fail to see the evil of such a passion:

8. Dalla Valle, p. 257.

Le Devoir et l'Amour avec trop de rigueur,
S'appliquent à la fois à déchirer mon cœur:
Je frémis tout ensemble et brûle pour ce crime,
La raison me gourmande et mon Amour m'opprime.

(39-42)

Making a supreme effort, Fauste "renonce par force à tant d'aimables charmes" (57) and decides to keep her love silent, even though such a "résolution me comble de douleurs" (59). But when she finds herself face to face with Chrispe, all these plans are forgotten. Like Phèdre, she tries to disguise her declaration of love, praising his valor and beauty:

Vous voyant si bien fait, et si vaillant encore,
La Thrace vous a pris pour le Dieu qu'elle adore,
Elle s'en va vous mettre au dessus des Autels,
Et placer votre Image entre les Immortels. (85-88)

Chrispe, not understanding her motives, returns the favor by suggesting that

tout l'honneur de cet heureux destin
Se doit attribuer au Sage Constantin, (91-92)

supposing that praise of the husband will please the wife. A second attempt only complicates the situation: when Fauste asks Chrispe to tell her of his victory, he speaks only of the valor of Licine, the vanquished foe. It is Fauste's turn to be puzzled: "Quoi? pour nos Ennemis avoir tant de clémence?" (177). Chrispe soon enlightens her: he loves Constance, Licine's daughter, who will soon arrive to plead the unfortunate family's case before Fauste. Thus, in spite of a brief *péripétie*, the situation remains unchanged: Chrispe still does not understand the situation. In fact, with her new knowledge, Fauste is in even deeper agony. In vain does she cast hints:

39

> Comment? à vous entendre on dirait qu'aujourd'hui
> Chrispe n'aurait plus rien à demander pour lui.
>
> (251-52)

Chrispe does not grasp the meaning of her subtle words. When she replies to his flattery by the doubly ironic line, "Vous voulez me séduire avec vos vanités" (283), his answer betrays only bumbling optimism, and the act ends in the same vein: Fauste's last attempt,

> Je ferai tout pour vous, et rien pour l'amour d'eux,
> Mon esprit n'agira que par votre prière,

brings about a rejoinder "carica di sinistri presagi":[9]

> Et bien, je prends sur moi la dette toute entière.
>
> (304-6)

As of that moment, the die is cast. By his obstinacy, his optimism, and because of his love—a love that excludes Fauste from the world of the two young lovers—Chrispe will not know of the terrible struggle going on in Fauste's heart and mind. He will, in effect, remain a stranger to the tragic events that engulf his world, so much so that even his death is little more than a horrible mistake. As Dalla Valle has so well pointed out, Fauste needs Chrispe, and her best lines are due to his presence. But Chrispe, in love with Constance, needs his stepmother only as a protector of the woman he loves. "La poesia di Chrispe si manifesta piuttosto di fronte a Constance."[10] Alone with Constance, Chrispe sings of a future happiness while Fauste, locked out, thinks only of destroying a rival that has "choqué ma gloire et mon amour" (1210).

Only one play, *Panthée*, defies our classification, and in so doing only strengthens our belief in the fact that the

---

9. Dalla Valle, p. 259.   10. Dalla Valle, p. 261.

psychological concepts described until now are basic to the theater of Tristan. Panthée is a stranger at the court of Cirus, but this is due neither to her birth nor to her acts: passive victim of war, she finds herself prisoner at the court of a monarch who does not understand her, entrusted to the care of a favorite who understands her even less. Thus, she is isolated in a world of hope and of illusion until reunited with her husband. In this play, therefore, we cannot speak of willful strangers, but rather of an *a priori* situation that forces certain characters to isolate themselves and thus to shut out others.

In the letter to Henry de Lorraine that precedes the play, Tristan mentions his struggle to regain "de la force et de la santé," and in the *avertissement* he describes himself as "languissant" in the throes of the illness that plagued him all his life. The sonnet "A Jésus-Christ, dans une maladie," which follows the play, depicts not only a man who is ill, but one whose physical ailments have definitely affected his morale. The play was a failure in every respect, and Tristan blames his illness, the "peu de matière" of the subject, and the death of Montdory, the famous actor for whose talents the play had been destined but who had been felled by a stroke during a performance of *Mariane* and was thus unable to create the role of Araspe. Tristan's illness may have been a legitimate excuse. The other two are not.[11]

According to Xenophon's *Cyropaedia*, Cyrus crushes the armies of the king of Assyria and takes many prisoners. Among them is the beautiful Panthea, wife of Abradates. Cyrus entrusts her to his friend Araspes who is confident that he will never become her slave since, according to him, love can always be ruled by the will. But, in spite of his will, he

11. There is no need here to comment on the many critiques of the play, from d'Aubignac's "Jugement de la tragédie intitulée Penthée, écrit sur le champ" to those of today; both Bernardin and Dalla Valle have done so satisfactorily.

succumbs and declares his love to Panthea who rejects him disdainfully and, when he threatens, complains to Cyrus. Like a true Solomon—though a somewhat ironic one—Cyrus settles the matter. Araspes feigns to flee from Cyrus' camp and the affair is never brought up again. Thus ends the first episode. In the second, Panthea assumes a far more tragic and touching role, a perfect model of conjugal fidelity. Grateful, and believing that she is to blame for Araspes' departure, a true loss to Cyrus, she decides to repay her benefactor by convincing her husband to change sides. In the very first battle, Abradates is killed and Panthea, faithful to the end, stabs herself and dies on the body of her husband.

Tristan is not dealing here with one meager subject, but with several subjects. Combining two episodes into one is not always easy, and it becomes impossible when the hero of one (Araspe) is nearly absent from the other. All the critics are in agreement: the weakest parts of the play are the fourth act and the denouement. How then could Montdory have saved the play as Araspe when, in that role, he would have spoken only four lines in Act IV, and twenty-four in the last two scenes of Act V? The subject is, in fact, to blame for the failure of the play, even if it is not sterile in every respect. As Bernardin has noted,[12] we are, from the very beginning, confronted with an untheatrical situation. There are three main characters, each one with his own theme, each one on a plane that will not permit him to become truly involved with the problems of his protagonists.

Cirus' theme is that of honor and glory. He considers himself "uno strumento della volontà divina su questa terra,"[13] and the entire first scene of the play is devoted to the pres-

12. Page 386.
13. Dalla Valle, p. 127.

entation of that theme. This attitude is put to its first test when the king faces Panthée in the second scene, but the king leaves no doubt in our minds:

> Cirus ayant su vaincre emportera la gloire
> D'avoir su noblement user de la victoire,
> En vous rendant l'honneur et la civilité
> Que veulent votre sexe et votre qualité. (127-30)

Cirus, in all of his actions, will be governed by the role that he expounds when he claims that a king must

> Gouverner son esprit ainsi que ses sujets,
> Et mêlant la justice à des bontés extrêmes,
> En commandant autrui, se commander soi-même.
> (190-92)

When Araspe opens his heart to Panthée, and when the queen complains to Cirus, the latter views these events only insofar as they shake his beliefs:

> Ma réputation se tache par ce crime,
> On en voit tout à coup décroître mon estime,
> Et de quelque façon qu'Araspe soit puni,
> L'éclat de ma grandeur en demeure terni. (883-86)

He is ready to punish the "insolent" when Panthée saves the situation:

> Sa faute est excusable, il faut que je le die,
> Après une cruelle et longue maladie
> Sa raison l'a quitté, son sens est affaibli,
> Vous mettrez s'il vous plaît cette faute en oubli:
> Je vous en veux prier. (1009-13)

With these words Panthée removes not only her demand for Araspe's punishment, but also any blemish on Cirus' honor: if Araspe's action was "excusable," it could not involve the

43

honor of his king. Abradate's friendship is accepted by Cirus, not in the spirit that it is meant, but because

> Les amis tels que vous apportent plus de gloire,
> Et plus d'utilité qu'une grande victoire.   (1267-68)

Yet it is this friendship that will be the weakness in Cirus' armor, for it is Abradate's death that shakes the faith that Cirus had in his attitude. Telling Panthée that

> Nous devions mettre ensemble, après ces grands combats,
> Les murs de Babylone et ceux de Sardes bas,   (1487-88)

he praises the dead hero only to reassure himself:

> Ton mérite toujours vivra dans ma mémoire,
> Et mille monuments élevés à ta gloire
> Se couvriront de marbre afin de faire foi
> Que j'eus beaucoup d'estime et d'amitié pour toi.
> (1497-1500)

Cirus leaves the sorrowful widow to pursue the enemy while, within a matter of minutes, Panthée and Araspe kill themselves. We do not know how this news will affect Cirus, for the play ends on precisely that question:

> Quel désastre! ô Cirus, comment l'apprendras-tu
> Sans que ce rude coup ébranle ta vertu?

These closing words of Hidaspe, suggesting that Cirus cannot fail to be "ébranlé" in this world where nothing is constant, find an echo in the motto that Tristan added after "Fin": "Nil Solidum."

Panthée, prisoner of Cirus, a queen enslaved, is surprised by the good treatment that she receives. This very surprise shows that Panthée, given over to her love for Abradate, understands neither Cirus nor his motives. Feeling indebted to her generous captor, she can think of only one way to repay him: assure him the services of her husband. D'Aubignac, in his critique of the play, thinks of Panthée as a woman motivated by chastity. Such cannot be the case, for it explains neither her desire to repay Cirus nor her clemency in saving Araspe. Rather, as Dalla Valle sees it, "per tutta la tragedia, Panthée non vibra che su questa sola corda": her love for her husband.[14] It is because of this love that she rejects Araspe, because of it that she feels indebted to Cirus who will reunite the lovers, because of it that, in her gratitude, she wishes to permit Cirus to forgive Araspe; and it is because of this love that she kills herself on the body of her beloved.

Throughout the first act Panthée speaks of her love and gratitude to friends who can only echo or to protagonists who, too involved in their own ideas, cannot truly communicate. Completely undramatic, this first act reveals Panthée as it did Cirus: a character so oblivious to problems that are not hers that she is unaware of the absence of true dialogue. Only in the second act does Panthée come face to face with a situation that has dramatic possibilities. Speaking of her love to one of her maids of honor,

O Dieux! si tu savais ce que c'est que d'aimer,
Quand d'un feu légitime on se sent enflammer,
(435-36)

she also tells her of her fears. In a passage in which joy and fear alternate, she utters some of the most lyrical lines of the play:

Le Soleil poursuivant la nuit aux voiles sombres,
A coups de traits dorés avait chassé les ombres,
Et les petits oiseaux que réveille l'amour
Célébraient en chantant la naissance du jour,
Lorsque ce songe affreux dont l'horreur m'épouvante

14. Dalla Valle, p. 127.

45

M'a fait voir d'Abradate une image vivante.
De ses vaines couleurs il me l'a si bien peint,
Que j'ai cru voir sa taille et ses yeux et son teint,
Le vrai ton de sa voix a frappé mon oreille,
Son visage était gai, sa bouche était vermeille,
Du bien de me revoir il rendait grâce aux Dieux,
Et son contentement se lisait dans ses yeux.
Mais comme je goûtais cette douceur extrême,
Je l'ai vu tout à coup triste, sanglant et blême. (465-78)

Her husband tells of his death in battle, ending his tale of horror with the admonition, "Fais que toujours au moins je vive en ta mémoire" (490). It is with these thoughts that she stumbles upon Araspe who, in an overly long and précieux tirade, bares his love for her. The scene could be as dramatic as the one in which Phèdre confesses her love to Hippolyte, but it fails, for the two protagonists never really communicate. Panthée's anger is prompted mainly by the fact that Araspe has not respected her "chastes amours" (636), and the latter does not truly understand—does he even hear?—her reproach. His answer shows plainly how wrong he is in his interpretation of Panthée's "A moi? parler d'amour?"

Je sais que pour atteindre au bonheur où j'aspire,
Il faut tenir au moins les rênes d'un Empire:
Mais le défaut d'un sceptre est un empêchement,
Que ma fidèle amour pourrait vaincre aisément.
Cirus comme il lui plaît élève les personnes,
Il dispense à son gré les fers et les couronnes.
Et de tant de faveur il daigne m'honorer
Que d'un Maître si grand je puis tout espérer.

(637-44)

Panthée's understanding is no greater: she only sees in him a man who offended her in her misfortune:

Il n'a pas redouté que sa faveur cessât.
Ni qu'il fût maltraité, pourvu qu'il m'offensât.
N'a-t-il pas entrepris, l'insolent et le traître,
D'aggraver mes malheurs en dépit de son maître?

(715-18)

Only when Charis, her maid of honor, points out that Panthée should squelch the affair for the sake of her own reputation, only when she points out that

On ne peut le punir qu'à votre préjudice:
Faut-il que le bruit coure en la bouche de tous

. . . .

Les plus sages du temps jamais ne se hasardent
A donner de l'éclat aux bruits qui les regardent,

(754-66)

does Panthée relent and decide to save Araspe from the wrath of Cirus.

Reunited with her husband, Panthée does not lapse into lyrics praising her love for him. Rather, having calmed his jealous fears, she prepares him to meet his new master and thus fulfill her covenant. It is thus that she presents him to Cirus:

Seigneur, de vos bienfaits voici le digne fruit,
Voilà cette Rançon que je vous ai promise,
Quand vos heureux succès m'ont ôté la franchise;
Vous m'avez bien traitée, et pour m'en revancher
Je vous offre un trésor que j'estime bien cher. (1246-50)

With the death of her beloved, Panthée sees her whole world crumble. For her, this is truly "la tragedia dell'illusione e della delusione."[15]

Many critics have blamed Tristan for the "baroque" ex-

15. Dalla Valle, p. 240.

tremes of Panthée's lamentations. In these, however, we see only the culmination of her entire poetic being:

> O charmante merveille! ô funeste prodige!
> C'est tout ce que j'adore, et tout ce qui m'afflige,
> C'est mon cher Abradate, et si ce ne l'est pas.
>
> (1432-34)

Blaming the Gods into whose care she had entrusted her husband, she gives in to her sorrow. Rejecting Cirus' offer of help, she sends everyone away, so as to be left alone with her dead husband, lamenting her fate and restating her love:

> Ton visage changé n'a point changé mon âme,
> Tu n'es plus rien que glace et je suis toute en flamme:
> Mon cœur est tout ouvert des coups qui t'ont blessé,
> Bien que tu sois parti, je ne t'ai point laissé;
> Mon esprit suit toujours ton ombre qui s'envole,
> Et ma bouche mourante à la tienne se colle.   (1593-98)

Blaming herself, she kills herself, but not before she has reaffirmed the constancy of her love in a world whose motto remains "Nil Solidum."

4. THE *EXCLUS:* HERODE AND LA FILLE DU MOUPHTI

Livie excuses all the past crimes of Auguste the man as well as all the future crimes of Auguste the emperor with these words:

> Tous ces crimes d'Etat qu'on fait pour la couronne,
> Le Ciel nous en absout alors qu'il nous la donne,
> Et dans le sacré rang où sa faveur l'a mis,
> Le passé devient juste et l'avenir permis.[1]

Ancient thrones had always been readily accessible to those with the courage to seize them, and Herod was little more than "a colossal parvenu."[2] Hardy, in creating the prototype of such a man, put Livie's thoughts in the mouth of one of Hérode's enemies: "Les appas d'un royaume autorisent le crime,"[3] and Du Ryer put it even more bluntly: "Les Sceptres sont à ceux qui peuvent les ravir."[4] Auguste in Corneille's *Cinna*, Phocas in his *Héraclius*, Arsace in Campistron's *Tiridate*, all show that when Hérode boasts of having risen by his own strength to his position, he is not an isolated phenomenon.

Tristan's Hérode has committed just as many crimes as Hardy's, but is far less monstrous, thanks particularly to the care taken by the author to explain the nature and motivation of the crimes involved. Mariane, speaking of her young brother, Aristobule, describes his physical and spiritual assets, adding that such graces could only have come from Heaven

1. Corneille, *Cinna*, ll. 1609-12.
2. Maurice Baudin, *The Profession of King in Seventeenth-Century French Drama* (Baltimore: Johns Hopkins Press, 1941), p. 38.
3. *Mariamne*, II.i.
4. *Dynamis*, I.i.

"Pour relever l'honneur des braves Machabées" (412). This view is obviously shared by the people:

> Le peuple que sa vue au Temple ravissait,
> Admirant ses appas, tout haut le bénissait.
>
> (417-18)

This, in the eyes of the seventeenth-century audience, justified his murder, for a king's first duty was to his self-preservation on the throne, and "if it is granted that the safe-guarding of his crown must be a king's first concern, the murder of Aristobule, for example, was an inescapable consequence of the young prince's popularity."[5]

As the play opens, Hérode addresses the murdered prince whose "fantôme injurieux" has troubled his sleep. Reassuring himself, he tells the ghost that

> Je suis assez savant en l'art de bien régner,
> Sans que ton vain courroux me le vienne enseigner;
> Et j'ai trop sûrement affermi mon Empire
> Pour craindre les malheurs que tu me viens prédire.
>
> (5-8)

His bravado fails to convince him, and he calls out for help. To his siblings who arrive at his call, he describes his nightmare, vividly recalling the features of the drowned Aristobule:

> Il semblait retiré de l'onde fraîchement,
> Son corps était enflé de l'eau qu'il avait bue,
> Ses cheveux tous mouillés lui tombaient sur la vue,
> Les flots avaient éteint la clarté de ses yeux,
> Qui s'étaient en mourant tournés devers les Cieux.
>
> (118-22)

But they also fail to calm his fears, and so he proceeds on his own, reminding himself that

5. Baudin, p. 39.

50

Tous les Asmonéens sont dedans le tombeau,
On voit dessus le Trône un Monarque nouveau,
Qui tient sous les lauriers sa Couronne et sa tête
Pour jamais à l'abri des coups de la tempête. (161-64)

If Hérode is a king anxious about his throne, he is no less
a husband anxious about his wife. However, he finds that
these two parts are not in harmony. Having boasted of his
valor, he seeks his siblings' pity by telling of Mariane's cold-
ness. To the taunts of his brother (239-42), he can only
reply that

L'erreur dont on m'accuse a troublé de grands hommes,
Soit aux siècles passés, soit au temps où nous sommes.
L'Amour est tellement fatal à la valeur,
Qu'il n'est point de Héros exempts de ce malheur.

(243-46)

Hérode's unhappiness is due in part to the fact that "Le feu
qui me consume, est un feu légitime," but also to the fact
that Mariane once cared for him. He has fought for his
throne, and God has helped him—"Il préserve ma tête, il
soutient ma couronne" (1095)—but where would he be
without Mariane?

Quand le Parthe inhumain prit Hyrcane et Phaselle[6]
Je dus ma délivrance à son conseil fidèle:
Sans cet insigne effet de sa secrète amour,
Je perdais à la fois, et le Sceptre, et le jour;
C'était fait de ma vie, et le traître Antigone,
En me foulant aux pieds, remontait sur le Trône.

(283-88)

Mariane is thus witness not only to the crimes of Hérode,
but also to the fact that, without her, he might not even be

6. In 40 B.C. Antigonus II Mattathias, with the aid of the Parthians, captured Herod, Hyrcanus, and Phasaël. Only Herod escaped unharmed, and
three years later, with the help of Mark Antony, became king of Judea.

51

king. His pride and his possessive love are both shaken by the disdainful rejection of the woman he adores and to whom he owes the very throne he is so proud of having secured. Hérode the lover and Hérode the king react simultaneously to Mariane's rejection, for they have become as one:

> Désormais de ta part tout me sera suspect,
> Je n'aurai plus pour toi ni bonté ni respect,
> Et s'il advient jamais que dans cette humeur noire,
> Tu lances quelque trait qui ternisse ma gloire,
> Je le repousserai d'un air qui fera foi,
> Qu'on ne doit pas manquer de respect à son Roi.
>
> (647-52)

And so, little by little, the gulf between husband and wife grows, thanks in part to the work of Hérode's siblings, thanks in part to the inability—or unwillingness—of the two major protagonists to communicate. According to seventeenth-century dramatic theory—and practice—"les personnes de naissance ne se portent qu'à de hauts desseins."[7] If history tells a different story, it is because "l'avis d'autrui corrompt leurs sentiments."[8] As his loneliness increases, Hérode seeks reasons for Mariane's aloofness. When he fails to understand her, he turns to his siblings for advice. However, since neither he nor they are "de naissance," the corruption of the siblings readily masters the scruples of the king. Later on, Hérode will blame Salomé and Phérore:

> Ministres de mes maux à me nuire obstinés,
> Vous m'osez consoler, vous qui m'assassinez?
> Vous m'avez fait donner par vos mauvais offices
> Cette atteinte mortelle à toutes mes délices,
> Vous m'avez inspiré ce funeste dessein,
> Vous m'avez fait entrer des bourreaux dans le sein.
>
> (1799-1804)

7. D'Aubignac, *La pratique du théâtre* (Paris: Champion, 1927), pp. 74-75.
8. Corneille, *Pompée*, l. 376.

But this is nothing more than an expected seventeenth-century commonplace,[9] one that heaps guilt upon the satellites without exonerating the principal villain.

That these satellites are not to be blamed for the catastrophe which ensues is made obvious by this fact: in every tragedy of Tristan, whatever evil advisors may suggest, the final decision takes shape only under the eyes of the eventual victim. This is equally true for many of Racine's plays, and mention of this phenomenon was made in the first chapter. Hérode, in the last scene of Act II, is on the verge of condemning Mariane, but his mind is not quite made up. But, when Mariane enters in the first scene of the following act, when Hérode feels judged himself by the provocative *regard* of the woman he plans to judge, then his fury knows no bounds. Thus when Hérode, looking at Mariane as a judge, sees that she is looking at him, when he feels that gaze and interprets it,

> Mais la voici qui vient avec autant d'audace,
> Que si je l'attendais pour implorer sa grâce:
> On dirait que l'altière en mesurant ses pas,
> Dépite ma justice, et brave le trépas.　　(751-54)

Hérode the judge is suddenly tranformed into Hérode the judged, and the inquisitor-turned-victim lashes out at his tormentor with a savagery born of frustration. Mariane's calm rejoinders, her continued insinuations recalling Hérode's past crimes,

> Mais jamais votre esprit n'a manqué d'artifice
> Pour perdre l'innocent sous couleur de justice,
> 　　　　　　　　　　　　　　　　　(771-72)

lead to the inevitable outburst: "La mort émoussera tous ces

9. For a full treatment of this commonplace, see Maurice Baudin, "The Shifting of Responsibility in Seventeenth-Century French Tragic Drama," *MLN*, XLIX (March, 1934), 152-58.

piquants propos" (773). Throughout this "trial," Mariane will refuse to play the game, not deigning even to answer the charges. To Hérode's angry "Il faut dénier ou confesser la chose" (808), she retorts with her usual pride and disdain:

> Par force ou par adresse il sera malaisé
> Qu'on me fasse avouer un crime supposé,
> Et n'était mes malheurs, je suis assez bien née
> Pour n'appréhender pas d'en être soupçonnée:
> Mon esprit que le Sort afflige au dernier point,
> Souffre les trahisons, mais il n'en commet point,
> Encore qu'il en eût un sujet assez ample,
> S'il était obligé de faillir par exemple.   (809-16)

The mention of these examples—"Le meurtre d'un Aïeul, l'assassinat d'un Frère" (819)—drives Hérode to utter insults which he can only regret, especially when, a few moments later, Mariane having melted into tears at the thought of her orphaned children, he finds himself imbued with "una folle speranza d'amore."[10] Inevitably, "La qualité de Roi cède à celle d'Amant" (894), and it is as lover that he utters the ironically lucid line "Vois de quelle façon mon sort dépend du tien" (905). This very line, however, opens the door to doubt and suspicion, for it reminds Mariane of the fact that Hérode had ordered her death in the event of his own. When Mariane voices these feelings, Hérode realizes that Soesme has betrayed him. He can think of only one reason for such a betrayal:

> Il n'a pas mis pour rien sa vie à l'aventure,
> Tu n'as pu l'éblouir par l'éclat des trésors,
> Tu n'as pu le tenter que par ceux de ton corps,
> Il en fut possesseur . . .   (1062-65)

When Mariane refuses to defend herself against this vile accusation—"Crois tout ce que tu dis, et tout ce que tu

10. Dalla Valle, p. 233.

penses" (1070)—he makes any reconciliation impossible by
his rejoinder:

> Oui, oui, je le veux croire, et te faire sentir,
> De cette perfidie un cuisant repentir.[11]   (1071-72)

If Mariane refuses to defend herself, Soesme does not. He
cannot understand how Hérode would think of such accusa-
tions:

> Peut-on croire qu'une âme et si noble et si belle,
> Conçoive des soupçons qui sont indignes d'elle,
>
>   (1133-34)

but his defense of Mariane only raises further questions in
Hérode's mind and he sends Soesme to the scaffold.

These decisions, as has been stated before, are taken in
the presence of the victim. Once they have been removed,
once Hérode no longer feels their judging eyes, then doubt
returns:

> Mais quoi, faire périr ce que j'ai tant aimé?
> Pourrai-je me résoudre à foudroyer un Temple
> Que j'ai tenu si cher et qui n'a point d'exemple?
> Mon esprit y résiste, et s'y trouve étonné.   (1244-47)

Only the persistent goading of Salomé and Phérore make
him say the fateful "Bien, qu'on l'ôte, qu'on l'ôte" which
seals Mariane's fate.

> Elle n'est plus au monde, ou bien l'on m'a trahi,
> Et c'est m'avoir perdu que m'avoir obéi.   (1421-22)

With these words, Hérode shows in the opening scene of
the last act that his mind is far from settled, that, like many

11. In La Calprenède's *Mort des enfants d'Hérode, ou suite de Mariane*,
Hérode condemns his own children in a like fashion. However, the two sons
are not simply proud, but arrogant, and unable, not unwilling, to escape and
save themselves.

of the baroque "almas doloridas, partidas en dos y que se pierden en inútiles esfuerzos para reunir las dos mitades irreductiblemente enemistadas,"[12] he is struggling with a problem whose macabre solution he already perceives. Alternating between moments of lucidity and moments of complete insanity, he calls upon Mariane to return to him, mourns her, curses himself for having caused her death, and then, having lost contact with reality, speaks to his court as though nothing had happened:

> C'est que j'ai trop de soin des affaires publiques,
> Mais je veux aujourd'hui prendre un peu de repos.
>
> .   .   .   .
>
> A parler librement, ce qui me tient en peine,
> C'est que depuis hier je n'ai point vu la Reine,
> Commandez de ma part qu'on la fasse venir.
>
> (1668-73)

A brief moment of sanity is filled with expressions of grief, but he soon lapses into his madness, seeking Mariane to "cercare ancora di stabilire con lei un contatto ora più che mai impossible":[13]

> Dites-lui de ma part qu'elle me vienne voir;
> Par sa seule présence elle cause ma joie,
> Je lui pardonne tout, pourvu que je la voie.
>
> (1738-40)

Narbal manages to bring him back to the world of reality, but not for long; Hérode, unable to rejoin his wife, gives her a new life: "Elle s'élève au Ciel pleine de Majesté" (1765). Too late he realizes that he cannot live without Mariane. Giving voice to his remorse, he thinks only of joining her:

---

12. A. Cioranescu, *El barroco o el descubrimiento del drama* (Tenerife: Universidad de la Laguna, 1957), p. 333.
13. Dalla Valle, p. 239.

Mon âme avec mes pleurs s'efforce de sortir.
Vois l'excès de l'ennui dont elle est désolée,
Et comment pour te suivre elle prend sa volée.

(1798-1800)

Fainting in the arms of his servants, he remains oblivious of the fact that death, in freeing Mariane from him, has forever separated them.

Gustave Larroumet could very well have been thinking of the Fille du Mouphti in *Osman* when he ended a lecture on Tristan with these words: "Avec lui nous voyons pour la première fois les événements du drame engendrés par les passions mêmes."[14] She is "uno dei più originalmente concepiti di tutto il suo teatro."[15]

When Fatime, the Sultane Sœur's slave, describes the Fille du Mouphti to Osman, she praises her beauty, but especially the "traits de son esprit" (181). She speaks of the young lady as being "modeste,/ Mais fière et pleine d'un orgueil/ A mettre d'un amant l'espérance au cercueil" (186-88). When Osman finally meets the Fille du Mouphti, he is immediately struck by "cette mine superbe" (428), but no less by the fact that he had put too much faith in the portrait: "En ce pinceau trompeur j'eus trop de confiance" (430). Coming to the conclusion that "elle a plus d'orgueil vingt fois que de beauté" (435), he rejects her before she has even the time to salute him.

Thus, the first words of the Fille du Mouphti are spoken at a moment when she has been rejected by the man she loves, when she considers herself

Une Fille à peu près sur le Trône placée,
Et qu'on a du Sérail indignement chassée.

(465-66)

14. "Histoire du théâtre français au XVIIᵉ siècle," *RCC*, XXV (1897), 359.
15. Dalla Valle, p. 264.

It is at this moment that the Fille du Mouphti will take on
the attitude and task that have caused so many critics to liken
her to Hermione:[16]

> Le Prophète là-haut n'aura point de puissance,
> Ou devant qu'il soit peu, j'en aurai la vengeance.
> Il aura contre lui tous les bons Musulmans,
> Les Anges, les humains, les Cieux, les Elements,
> Et n'eût-il que moi seule à sa mort préparée,
> Qu'il sache que sa vie est fort mal assurée.   (481-86)

With Selim she plots the overthrow of the proud Osman,
promising—by implication (555-60)—to personally reward
the dissatisfied bassa once his task is accomplished: "Je con-
naîtrai ton cœur quand je verrai sa tête" (558). Yet in spite
of that promise which she repeats to herself in her *stances*
at the opening of Act III, she, like Hermione plotting with
Oreste, knows that she cannot reward Selim, for "mon cœur
n'est plus à donner" (643). In spite of her well-nurtured
hatred she still loves Osman, as she reluctantly admits after
a thorough self-examination:

> Tu l'aimes? oui je l'aime: et bien, qu'en veux-tu dire,
> Raison, qui sur mon âme a pris un tel empire,
> Que dans les mouvements du plus grand déplaisir,
> Tu ne lui laisses pas l'usage du désir?
> Oui! j'aime ce cruel, oui, j'aime ce barbare,
> Et confesse toujours que son mérite est rare;
> Je trouve que sa mine éblouit tous les yeux,
> Qu'il semble que ce Prince est descendu des Cieux,
> Comme un brillant éclair, comme un foudre de guerre,
> Capable de dompter tous les cœurs de la terre.   (658-67)

And it is only with the greatest of efforts that she decides
to "demeurer toujours aux termes du devoir" (697). Having

16. The parallel is obvious and has been thoroughly commented by such
eminent critics as Bernardin, *op. cit.*, and Jean Pommier, *Aspects de Racine*
(Paris: Nizet, 1954).

momentarily lost faith in the ability of Selim to avenge her, she, like Hermione, decides that her own hand "vengera mon injure" (839).

During the entire fourth act Osman fights for his throne and his life, and the Fille du Mouphti remains off-stage. Only in the last act, when Osman has lost his throne, does she reappear. Osman, seeing her enter, shows by his reaction that his misfortune has not changed his character:

> Cieux! qu'est-ce que je vois, cette fille importune
> Accroît par son objet ma mauvaise fortune;
> Ne prenons pas la route où ses pas sont tournés,
> Ou passons promptement le mouchoir sur le nez.
>
> (1308-11)

Attempting to express her pity for him, she only antagonizes Osman with her reproaches and her reminder that she could have saved him:

> Et salue en passant la fille d'un Mouphti
> Qui de tant de malheurs t'aurait bien garanti,
> Si tu n'eusses troublé la paix de sa famille,
> En faisant un éclat au mépris de sa fille.   (1314-17)

She errs in prolonging her tirade, listing her complaints, and when she compounds that error by gloating, the stichomythic duel that ensues leaves her no choice but to retreat:

> Tu vois quel est le sort que t'a fait ton caprice.
> Que me peux-tu répondre en ce funeste jour?
>
> OSMAN
> Que je trouve mes maux plus doux que ton amour.
>
> LA FILLE DU MOUPHTI
> J'aurais par mon amour affermi ta Puissance.
>
> OSMAN
> Ce mal aurait possible accablé ma constance.

La Fille du Mouphti
Mon amour en ta bouche un mal se peut nommer!

Osman
Je penserais plutôt à mourir qu'à t'aimer.   (1329-35)

Realizing the error of her approach, she changes course:

Seigneur! par ces rigueurs tu punis mon audace,
Qui trop insolemment s'attache à ta disgrâce:
Aussi t'oser blâmer durant cette saison,
C'est manquer de courage autant que de raison.
Pardonne-moi ce crime, ô Prince magnanime!
Si ce premier transport peut passer pour un crime,
Tu sais bien que mon Sexe a trop de vanité
Pour être sans dépit quand il est rebuté.   (1336-43)

In lines worthy of Racine she pours out her love. She wanted vengeance while he was on the throne, and were he still ruler, she would not hesitate to pursue it, but now that he has lost everything, she can only think of her love for him. The fact that she still loves him, she points out, must surely show that ambition was not her prime motive.

Mais sur ces sentiments ne t'imagine pas
Que ta grandeur passée eut sur moi des appas.
Je trouvais ta personne encore plus précieuse,
Et je ne t'aimais point comme une ambitieuse.
De peur que ton esprit ne soit en quelque erreur,
J'aimais Osman lui-même et non pas l'Empereur,
Et je considérais en ta noble personne
Des brillants d'autre prix que ceux de ta couronne.
(1362-69)

If she were queen and Osman a simple soldier, "Il n'aurait qu'à m'aimer et tout serait à lui" (1375). Osman is touched, but his mind is not on love: the danger is pressing and he must leave to defend his honor and his throne. Refusing the help of the Fille du Mouphti, who suggests her rooms as a hiding place, he goes to face the rebels. Once again, she finds herself left out. Too late, she realizes that he will never love her, but that she will always love him:

> Il ne me peut souffrir, il me hait, il m'abhore,
> Il me quitte, il me fuit, et si je l'aime encore.[17]
>
> . . . .
>
> Que n'ai-je été pour toi sans oreille, sans yeux,
> Sans orgueil, sans courroux, sans esprit, sans adresse,
> Sans soupirs et sans pleurs, ou plutôt sans tendresse?
>
> (1396-1411)

Deciding to follow him into danger, she vows to die for him, hoping to "périr à sa vue" (1419) but, prompted by Fatime, she explains at length the birth of her love and, by the time her long speech is over, Osman is dead.[18] Thus, the Fille du Mouphti, like so many other heroes and heroines of Tristan shut out by the ones they love, seeks in death the union that has eluded her in life. In her last lines, Bernardin sees little but précieux melodrama, but Dalla Valle points out very clearly that here, "assistiamo, come già altre volte, al riscatto attraverso l'ispirazione dell'intellettualistica ricercatezza figurative barocca, e in questo senso ci pare che essi coronino degnamente, contrariamente all'opinione del Bernardin, l'evoluzione del personaggio più poeticamente valido della tragedia."[19]

17. It should be kept in mind that *et si* was used as *et pourtant* in the seventeenth century.
18. This wordy tirade seems totally out of place here, and it was obviously added by Tristan to allow enough time for the death, off-stage, of Osman.
19. Page 266.

5. THE *EXCLUS:* ARASPE, NERON, FAUSTE

While Hérode and the Fille du Mouphti feel themselves rejected from the start, such is not the case of the three heroes that remain to be discussed. It may be obvious to the reader that at least two of them—Araspe and Fauste —are never a part of the world in which they wish to dwell, but this truth dawns on each of these protagonists only little by little, and too late.

In the original version of *Panthée,* as it was first played, Araspe's fate was not decided. D'Aubignac blamed this and, some time before the first edition of the play, Tristan reworked the denouement to allow Araspe to follow Panthée's example. While this new conclusion may have satisfied d'Aubignac and Richelieu—at whose request d'Aubignac had criticized the play—it does nothing but detract from the poetic unity of Tristan's original creation.

Throughout the play Araspe functions on a single plane, that of lover. It is interesting that his name is not among those of the other participants at the head of the second scene of the play, the first in which Araspe appears. Simple oversight? Probably, but Araspe remains quiet until Cirus entrusts Panthée into his care with these words:

> Araspe, fais toujours avec un soin extrême
> Qu'on respecte Madame à l'égal de moi-même.

As he exits, his ambiguous reply,

> Sire, on ne saurait voir ce miracle des Cieux
> Sans lui rendre aussitôt l'honneur qu'on doit aux Dieux,
> (219-22)

heightens the impression that he not only is not part of the conversation, but also that he does not grasp the full meaning of the words that have been exchanged.

Two scenes later, face to face with Panthée, Araspe will again be in a position to reveal his love, and again he will veil his declaration:

PANTHEE
Cirus est un miracle en rares qualités
Qu'on ne doit comparer qu'à des divinités.

ARASPE
Madame, dans ce rang vous pourriez prendre place.

PANTHEE
Vous voulez, me flattant, adoucir ma disgrâce;
C'est en continuant vos soins accoutumés,
Avec beaucoup d'esprit, montrer que vous m'aimez.

ARASPE
On ne peut rien aimer qui soit plus adorable.   (257-63)

Several lines later, he nearly faints at the mere mention of his rival, Abradate. Thus it is throughout the play: Araspe considers himself a legitimate suitor, refuses to understand that he is not truly Abradate's rival, and never quite faces the fact that there is no place for him in Panthée's world, although he confesses to Charis, Panthée's maid of honor, that,

Un destin tout-puissant, une invincible Etoile
Aux yeux de ma Raison attache un sombre voile.
Je sais bien que je sers une ingrate Beauté,
Et qu'aimant sans espoir, j'ai des feux sans clarté.
(327-30)

In the *stances* that open the second act, Araspe, finding no solace in the camp of Cirus, tells his woes to the forest:

63

> Hôtes du silence et de l'ombre,
> Où l'air est si frais et si sombre,
> Arbres qui connaissez l'état de ma langueur,
> Soyez les confidents des peines que j'endure,
> Et souffrez que je grave en votre écorce dure
> Le beau nom que l'Amour a gravé dans mon cœur.[1]
>
> (341-46)

In lines reminiscent of those of Hérode, who also felt his unrequited love and whose lyricism has few equals in the seventeenth century, Araspe deplores the fact that Panthée is "ingrate et cruelle" (377), and "Que jamais sa pitié récompense ma foi" (385). Abradate alone "est l'objet de toutes ses pensées" (390). Araspe sees in Abradate little more than a rival, an

> Ennemi de mon bien, obstacle de ma joie,
> Que le Sort enrichit d'une si belle proie,

and he decides to fight for such a worthy prize:

> je veux t'aller chercher,
> Et l'épée à la main te la faire lâcher.   (397-400)

In a moment of lucidity, he realizes that "Panthée est à la fois sa femme et son Amante" (406), but this wisdom is fleeting, and moments later he again searches for "Un secret pour lui plaire et pour me contenter" (420).

When, at last, he bares his feelings in a long declaration of love (545-628), when he soars on the wings of his emotional outburst, he loses all contact with reality. Panthée's violent reaction, already discussed at the end of Chapter 3, makes him aware of the fact that she does not understand him; but he does not realize that he does not understand her either. When, rejected and misunderstood, he fails to

1. For a fuller treatment of Tristan's use of nature, see my article "Un poète de la nature au dix-septième siècle: Tristan L'Hermite," FR, XXXIV (October, 1964), 51-59.

understand—or to justify—Panthée's reaction, he indulges in a long (sixty-one lines) monologue during which Tristan reaches "la sua più autentica ispirazione,"[2] and this is because Araspe "ha una sua ragion d'essere poetica soltanto fino al momento in cui si dichiara a Panthée e ne è respinto."[3] At no time does he feel guilty, and he is willing to face Cirus' ire without trepidation. Panthée's intervention in his favor—which he appreciates, but whose motives he does not understand—only strengthens this feeling, for he refuses to believe that he has done anything wrong:

> Hé, Sire, à l'offenser je n'ai jamais pensé;
> Les Cieux me sont témoins que je suis l'offensé.
>
> (1031-32)

This impression is accentuated by his triumphal—repugnantly so—statements that open the last act. He has just heard of Abradate's death, and rejoices at the thought:

> Selon mes vœux secrets il a perdu la vie,
>
> .   .   .   .
>
> Que la terre ô grands Dieux! soit légère à ses os,
> Pourvu que mon bonheur succède à son repos,
> Et qu'après ce grand deuil qu'on fait sur sa disgrâce
> Je sois assez heureux pour occuper sa place.   (1317-30)

But Oronte, relating the sad events, also brings bad news to the star-crossed lover: Panthée,

> A qui cette nouvelle aussitôt fut portée,
> L'enleva sur un char avec un si grand deuil,
> Qu'on les mettra tous deux dans un même cercueil,
> Car elle fait bien voir qu'elle n'a pas d'envie
> De survivre longtemps la moitié de sa vie.   (1402-6)

Oronte, in fact, has foreseen what the "trop facile Araspe" and the "Cirus trop crédule" did not; namely, that the

2. Dalla Valle, p. 244.   3. Dalla Valle, p. 241n.

death of Abradate was not a beginning, but an end, that this very death, rather than permitting new hope, ended it forever. Panthée, still faithful *amante*, follows her husband and lover to the tomb, shutting out Araspe with greater finality than ever. Araspe follows Panthée in an attempt to show that

> Malgré tous les efforts de ton cruel orgeuil
> Je te veux adorer au delà du cercueil,
> Et donner par ce coup une preuve évidente
> Que contre mon amour la mort est impuissante.
>
> (1647-50)

However, while the gesture may well prove his love, it opens no new vistas, and if the world of the living is ruled by the omnipresent "nil solidum," that of the dead is static, and Araspe fails to achieve in death that which he sought in life.

Dalla Valle, in her treatment of *La mort de Sénèque*, states that all eleven characters are important and are "osservati nel momento in cui si stabilise fra di loro un qualche rapporto." [4] I would rather suggest that they are important insofar as they point out the complete impossibility of any real relationship. From the start, Néron—like Hérode— asserts that he is ruler of a world that he wishes to share with Sabine: "Enfin, selon mes vœux, Sabine est sans rivale" (1). But, unlike Hérode, Néron does not see himself excluded from the start. Rather, he and Sabine seek absolute power and wealth while also desiring universal approval. Thus, unlike Hérode, who finds himself shut out by his wife from the start, Néron sees hostility grow around him as his policy—or rather, that of his wife—alienates those whose vote of confidence he most desires.

4. Pages 248-49.

Since even he cannot visualize public acceptance of his policies, Néron must be reassured by Sabine. Thus, the entire first act is taken up by his attempts at justifying his past and future misdeeds. When, in Act III, Néron confronts Epicaris, he does not question her as though she were seeking a personal revenge:

> Apprends-moi qui t'anime et qui te désespère;
> Ai-je ravi tes biens, ou fait périr ton père,
> Entrepris sur ta vie, ou bien sur ton honneur,
> Et de quelque façon traversé ton bonheur?   (747-50)

He wants to be accepted, to be honored, and can never forgive Epicaris for voicing the general discontent:

> Oui, je sais le dessein de cent hommes d'honneur
> Qui fondent sur ta mort leur souverain bonheur.
> (1709-10)

Sabine and Néron face the wrath of Epicaris who judges them to the end:

NERON
Prends-tu quelque plaisir à te faire gêner?

EPICARIS
Beaucoup moins qu'un Tiran n'en goûte à l'ordonner.

SABINE
L'impudente, la terre est-elle bien capable
De porter un moment ce Monstre insupportable?

EPICARIS
Elle peut sans horreur porter Epicaris,
Puisqu'elle porte bien la femme aux trois maris.

SABINE
Ta langue pour ce mot sera bientôt coupée.

EPICARIS
Que devrait-on couper à Sabine Popée?

67

SABINE

Quand tu n'aurais vomi que ce mot seulement,
Tu mourras de cent morts par mon commandement.

EPICARIS

Ces matières de peur sont ce que je dédaigne:
Menace-moi plutôt de vivre sous ton règne;
Aucun autre malheur ne me saurait troubler,
Et c'est la seule peur qui me ferait trembler.

NERON

O nouvelle Alecton que l'Enfer a vomie!
Qui t'a donné sujet d'être mon ennemie?
Qui de ta cruauté me rend ainsi l'objet?

EPICARIS

Tu veux donc le savoir, en voici le sujet:
Je t'aimais autrefois, quand ton front hypocrite
Se couvrait faussement des couleurs du mérite;

. . . .

Mais depuis que tu cours où la fureur te guide,
Que tu te rends cruel, ingrat, et parricide,
Que tu rôdes la nuit, et que tu tiens à jeu,
Les titres de voleur et ceux de boute-feu,
Je te hais comme un Monstre abîmé dans le crime,
Et trouve que ta mort est un coup légitime.

(1713-44)

It is this judgment that dooms Epicaris, but it is also this judgment which is followed immediately by the relation of the death of Sénèque, a death which is, in itself, a judgment. As the centurion tells of Sénèque's death, the truth dawns on Néron at last. He realizes that

Tous mes sens sont troublés, et mon âme inquiète
Ne peut plus se remettre en sa première assiette.

(1846-47)

He senses his error, senses that the world condemns him, and, in fact, condemns himself, though he does not quite know why. Only Sabine is left at his side, but Néron, shut out, realizes at last that she is the one person who cannot help him:

> Ah! ne me parles point.
> Eloignes-toi d'ici, fuis promptement, Sabine,
> De peur que ma colère éclate à ta ruine.   (1861-63)

Alone at last, Néron reaches his poetic potential in the final lines of the play, and hurls to Heaven the challenge already cited in Chapter 3: "Mais avant, je perdrai la moitié de la Terre" (1867). For the first time, he realizes that he is truly "solo di fronte al destino e di fronte a se stesso." [5]

Unlike Phèdre, Fauste never reaches the moment of open declaration. Phèdre will hint of her love, but when Hippolyte fails to grasp the meaning of this indirect language, Phèdre unleashes her passions: "Hé bien! connais donc Phèdre et toute sa fureur" (673). Fauste will never open her heart, and there will never be any true communication between her and any other character in the play. In fact, from the very beginning, La mort de Chrispe is a tragedy of errors in which malentendus and quid pro quos rule a world of absurdity.

Fauste never declares herself to anyone, for she cannot share the horrible burden that she bears. Thus, Chrispe never really shuts her out. Rather, she is shut out by her own conscience. With great strength of will she rejects the idea of confessing her love (1-62), but all this strength disappears in the presence of the beloved. No sooner does Fauste hear of Chrispe's approach than she begins to abandon her resolve:

5. Dalla Valle, p. 251.

69

Ah Chrispe, il peut entrer.
Mais suis-je en un état à me pouvoir montrer?
Demeure Cornélie; ô Dieux, à cette vue
On me verra changer, je serai toute émue;
Je devrais éviter ce fatal entretien:
Retourne, et lui dis que. . . . Mais non, ne lui dis rien.
Va donc; arrête encore. . . .   (67-73)

It is this indecision that is manifest in the third scene described in Chapter 3: Fauste hints of a passion that Chrispe
never really discovers. As Act I ends, Fauste knows more
about Chrispe than before, but this new knowledge only
makes her love more difficult to divulge. From that moment
on, she feels shut out, not by Chrispe, but by the circumstances and by her own conscience. In the *stances* that open
Act II, it is this very problem that she thinks over.

Fauste, à quoi te résoudras-tu
Entre l'Amour et la Vertu
Qui tiennent aujourd'hui ton âme balancée?
Déjà la Crainte et le Désir
Font des ligues dans ta pensée;
Il faut laisser ou prendre, il est temps de choisir.
                    (307-12)

She is aware of her duty, but "mon Ame est encline où
le péril est grand" (318). Unlike Phèdre, Fauste realizes that
her guilt does not depend on her revelation of it. At first
there is doubt in her mind, and she asks herself a question
to which the Bible—Matthew 5:28—provides the answer:

Quel crime en ces pensers si je cache ma flamme?
Toute l'horreur du Crime a sa source dans l'âme.
                    (357-58)

Like Phèdre, she is on the point of resignation when she
finds out that her worst fears are indeed fact: Constance
and Chrispe love each other. Giving vent to her fury, she
swears that

70

Nous lèverons le masque à sa trompeuse flamme:
Nous saurons éclairer jusqu'au fond de son Ame,
Et nous lui ferons voir, s'il prétend s'échapper,
Qu'il est trop jeune encor pour nous vouloir tromper.

(389-92)

This position might be compared to that of Araspe who, excluded from the world of Panthée and Abradate, sees himself as "wronged," but it should be remembered that Fauste, as empress seeing an enemy of the state protected by a national hero, has a right to feel offended. The question then is not whether or not Fauste has the right to resent Chrispe's love, but whether or not that resentment exists for the proper reason. It is true that Fauste offers her support to Chrispe if he abandons "et Licine, et les siens" (910), but this is not prompted by political motives. Her last lines in Act III, spoken to her *confidente*, show that she is quite willing to put her position at the service of her love:

FAUSTE

Je l'y forcerai bien, s'il ne plie, il rompra,
Il quittera l'Empire, ou changera de flamme.

CORNELIE

Mais il est Fils d'Auguste.

FAUSTE

Et moi j'en suis la femme,
Et nous verrons bientôt, s'il me veut mettre au pis,
Lequel l'emportera de la femme, ou du fils.   (970-74)

She proceeds to win the emperor over to her point of view and, ironically, it is at that point that Chrispe enters to express his gratitude for all that Fauste has done for the young lovers. His speeches only reaffirm his position and heighten the fury of Fauste. To make matters worse, Constance

71

follows on her lover's heels, echoing his thoughts. Constance speaks of Licine's errors and of Fauste's clemency. The latter soon enlightens Constance: Licine sinned against the Empire, and this can be forgiven. Constance, however, indulged in a far more dangerous game, one which Fauste cannot overlook:

Si Licine en fuyant est sorti de la Thrace,
Vous l'avez sur le champ vengé de bonne grâce:
Exprimant un pouvoir qui n'est point limité,
Vous avez mis aux fers celui qui l'a dompté.

. . . .

Chrispe vous rend des soins et vous fait les doux yeux,
Vous obsède à toute heure et vous suit en tous lieux.

(1159-74)

When she fails to shake Constance's faith in Chrispe, Fauste reveals her plans:

FAUSTE

Enfin, quoi qu'il en soit, Constance n'est point née
Pour prétendre avec Chrispe au lien d'Hyménée:
Nous ne souffrirons point qu'il soit fait son Epoux.

CONSTANCE

Vous souffrirez au moins qu'il m'aime mieux que vous.

FAUSTE

A son dam s'il vous aime, interdit de le faire.

CONSTANCE

A son dam beaucoup plus s'il agit au contraire.

FAUSTE

Il ne peut vous aimer qu'avec beaucoup d'erreur.

CONSTANCE

Ni vous aimer aussi qu'avec beaucoup d'horreur.

72

FAUSTE

Ah! sortez promptement, engeance de vipère.

CONSTANCE

On ne m'accuse point d'avoir perdu mon Père.[6]

(1191-1200)

The truth of these last two sallies is too much for Fauste, and she decides that Constance must die:

> L'insolente qu'elle est, voit encore le jour
> Après avoir choqué ma gloire et mon amour?
>
> (1209-10)

It has been suggested that Fauste does not act because of her passion, rather that it is "sa rage d'être combattue politiquement dans l'âme de Constantin qui la fait éclater contre Chrispe."[7] But the long—over one hundred lines—tirade that follows can be boiled down to two of its most powerful lines:

> Plutôt que cette Amour m'offense impunément,
> Je veux perdre à la fois et l'Amante et l'Amant.
>
> (1241-42)

In fact, it is Chrispe who is her rival in Constantin's heart, and it is Chrispe who will be spared:

> Ne fais rien qui t'oblige à des grandes douleurs,
> Et préviens sagement tes soupirs et tes pleurs.
>
> (1269-70)

Pitiless in her hatred, Fauste directs all her venom against Constance, and justifies herself coldly:

6. In 310, three years after her marriage to Constantine, Fausta denounced her father who had tried to obtain her help in an attempt on Constantine's life.

7. André Stegmann, "Les métamorphoses de Phèdre," in *Actes du Premier Congrès International Racinien* (Uzès: Péladan, 1962), p. 50.

> En m'osant offenser, Constance s'est perdue.
> La mort qu'elle reçoit est une peine due,
> Ma violence est juste et n'a rien d'inhumain,
> Elle dicte l'Arrêt la balance à la main.   (1403-6)

But, as we have stated before, this is a tragedy of errors,
and Fauste's vengeance backfires. Learning of the death of
the young lovers, she refuses to blame herself:

> O Destins! ô Venins! ô Mort! ô Violence!
> Que ne laissez-vous Chrispe en enlevant Constance.
>
> .   .   .   .
>
> Quoi? si je lance un trait, ô rigoureuse loi,
> Pour me percer le cœur il réfléchit sur moi? (1543-50)

In her sorrow, she realizes that Constance and Chrispe are
now forever united in death:

> Par ce funeste trait qui ne m'a point vengée,
> J'ai servi ma Rivale et me suis outragée.
> Constance a de ce mal retiré mille biens,
> Chrispe a fermé ses yeux, elle a fermé les siens,
> Et serrant les liens dont l'Amour les assemble,
> Ils ont fait leurs adieux et sont partis ensemble.
> Pour rendre mon dépit et plus juste et plus grand,
> On les a vus encor s'embrasser en mourant:
> En un sang qui se glace ils conservent des flammes,
> Leurs corps restent unis aussi bien que leurs âmes;
> La Mort ne défait pas ce que l'Amour a joint.
> Ils quittent la lumière et ne se quittent point:
> Chrispe baise en mourant Constance qui l'adore,
> Ils n'ont plus de chaleur, et s'ils brûlent encore:
> Leur dessein continue au delà du trépas,
> Et dans leur cœur éteint leur amour ne l'est pas.
> (1551-66)

Remorseless, she sees this death as the supreme insult to

74

her love. Feeling shut out, she seeks death, not as a liber-
ating force, but as the means to seek once more that which
has eluded her so far:

> Ah Constance! c'est trop traverser mon envie.
>
> .   .   .   .
>
> Je te veux suivre encore, et chercher une voie
> Pour rompre tes plaisirs et traverser ta joie;
> Je veux troubler encor ton amoureux dessein,
> Te porter des flambeaux et des fers dans le sein,
> Et m'opposant là-bas à ton Idolatrie,
> Au milieu des damnés te servir de furie.   (1567-76)

CONCLUSION

The titles of the preceding chapters, along with an occasional reference to *L'Etranger*, may tend to suggest that the tragic world of Tristan L'Hermite is populated by Meursaults. This was not intended. In fact, if a connection with Camus is to be made, it might well be with the statement which he made at the Dominican convent of Latour-Maubourg in 1948: "Ce que j'ai envie de vous dire aujourd'hui, c'est que le monde a besoin de vrai dialogue, que le contraire du dialogue est aussi bien le mensonge que le silence, et qu'il n'y a donc de dialogue possible qu'entre des gens qui restent ce qu'ils sont et qui parlent vrai." [1]

The Hérodes of Tristan's tragedies seek such a dialogue which is made impossible by themselves as much as by the Marianes who torment them. When dialogue with others becomes impossible, these characters lapse into a state of self-deception consecrated by madness and stilled only by death. In this state, lucidity seldom comes to them or, if it does, it comes too late to stem the tide of events precipitated by the original *malentendu*.

Under these circumstances, the key figure in each play may well be the one whose name the play bears, but it is highly debatable whether that figure is the most dramatic. In fact, while Mariane, Panthée, Sénèque, Chrispe, or Osman are the central figures of the plays discussed, while they are the nuclei of the tragedies bearing their names, they are obviously not the most tragic.

Tristan seems to be at his best when he allowed rejected love to express its sorrow or its rage, for his forte was poetry, and it was to the lyricism of those shut out by the aforementioned key figures that many of the plays owed a large part of their original success.

1. *Actuelles* (Paris: Gallimard, 1950), p. 213.

UNIVERSITY OF FLORIDA MONOGRAPHS

Humanities

No. 1: *Uncollected Letters of James Gates Percival*, edited by Harry R. Warfel

No. 2: *Leigh Hunt's Autobiography: The Earliest Sketches*, edited by Stephen F. Fogle

No. 3: *Pause Patterns in Elizabethan and Jacobean Drama*, by Ants Oras

No. 4: *Rhetoric and American Poetry of the Early National Period*, by Gordon E. Bigelow

No. 5: *The Background of The Princess Casamassima*, by W. H. Tilley

No. 6: *Indian Sculpture in the John and Mable Ringling Museum of Art*, by Roy C. Craven, Jr.

No. 7: *The Cestus. A Mask*, edited by Thomas B. Stroup

No. 8: *Tamburlaine, Part I, and Its Audience*, by Frank B. Fieler

No. 9: *The case of John Darrell: Minister and Exorcist*, by Corinne Holt Rickert

No. 10: *Reflections of the Civil War in Southern Humor*, by Wade H. Hall

No. 11: *Charles Dodgson Semeiotician*, by Daniel F. Kirk

No. 12: *Three Middle English Religious Poems*, edited by R. H. Bowers

No. 13: *The Existentialism of Miguel de Unamuno*, by José Huertas-Jourda

No. 14: *Four Spiritual Crises in Mid-Century American Fiction*, by Robert Detweiler

No. 15: *Style and Society in German, Literary Expressionism*, by Egbert Krispyn

No. 16: *The Reach of Art: A Study in the Prosody of Pope*, by Jacob H. Adler

No. 17: *Malraux, Sartre, and Aragon as Political Novelists*, by Catharine Savage

No. 18: *Las Guerras Carlistas y el Reinado Isabelino en la Obra de Ramón del Valle-Inclán*, por María Dolores Lado

No. 19: *Diderot's Vie de Sénèque: A Swan Song Revised*, by Douglas A. Bonneville

No. 20: *Blank Verse and Chronology in Milton*, by Ants Oras

No. 21: *Milton's Elisions*, by Robert O. Evans

No. 22: *Prayer in Sixteenth-Century England*, by Faye L. Kelly

No. 23: *The Strangers: The Tragic World of Tristan L'Hermite*, by Claude K. Abraham

E DUE